FUNERARY URN FROM A ZAPOTECAN TOMB

The cylindrical urn is concealed behind the human figure. The dress of the human figure consists of a cape, apron, and a widespreading headdress. Over the face is worn a mask. Height, 15½ inches.

Ancient Civilizations of Mexico and Central America

HERBERT J. SPINDEN

INTRODUCTION BY

BRUCE E. BYLAND

LEHMAN COLLEGE AND THE GRADUATE CENTER,
CITY UNIVERSITY OF NEW YORK

DOVER PUBLICATIONS, INC.
Mineola, New York

Bibliographical Note

This Dover edition, first published in 1999, is an unabridged republication of the third and revised edition of the work originally published in 1928 by the Anthropological Handbook Fund of the American Museum of Natural History, New York. A new Introduction has been specially prepared for this edition.

Please note that this Dover reprint of *Ancient Civilizations of Mexico and Central America* retains the pagination of the original edition cited above in which the main text begins on page 5. There are no missing pages.

Library of Congress Cataloging-in-Publication Data

Spinden, Herbert Joseph, 1879–1967.
   Ancient civilizations of Mexico and Central America / Herbert J. Spinden ; introduction by Bruce E. Byland.
      p.   cm.
   Originally published: Third and rev. ed. New York : American Museum of Natural History, 1928, in series: Handbook series ; no. 3.
   Includes bibliographical references (p.   ) and index.
   ISBN 0-486-40902-3 (pbk.)
   1. Indians of Mexico—Antiquities. 2. Mexico—Antiquities. 3. Indians of Central America—Antiquities. 4. Central America—Antiquities.   I. Title.
F1219.S767   1999
972'.01—dc21   99-39030
                                                                                      CIP

Manufactured in the United States of America
Dover Publications, Inc., 31 East 2nd Street, Mineola, N.Y. 11501

INTRODUCTION TO THE DOVER EDITION

In 1917, Herbert Spinden published the first edition of the book that is here reprinted. It was, in that year, a monumental work of synthesis. Before it, few attempts had been made to present a unified prehistory of the entire region that was to become known as Mesoamerica. Most of the scholarship of the previous decades had been devoted to the study of particular regions or particular cultures of ancient Mexico (cf. Morley 1915, Prescott 1843, Spinden 1913, Stephens 1841). Earlier efforts at regional integration had only occasionally been undertaken by scholars like T. A. Joyce (1914), C. Lumholtz (1902), A. Peñafiel (1890), and E. Seler (1902–8), among others. Spinden's work, though not the most scholarly, was by far the most successful in reaching a popular audience. Designed from the start as a concise survey of the whole region, it presented authoritative information in a well organized and easily readable form. As with any ambitious project, the original edition of this volume prompted some criticism, and so it was revised and improved in each of the later editions (cf. Beyer 1918). It is the third and revised edition, published in 1928, that is here reprinted. A final revision was published as part of *Maya Art and Civilization* in 1957.

Today, Herbert Spinden's many contributions to the field of Mesoamerican art and archaeology are often undervalued, as are his efforts as a humanist who affirmed the worth of all people—whatever their race or ethnic background. Important discussions of Spinden's life and his contributions to Mesoamerican scholarship can be found in Brunhouse (1975), Wauchope (1965), and Willey and Sabloff (1974).

The Life and Work of Herbert Joseph Spinden

Spinden was born in 1879 in Huron, South Dakota. Herbert's father, a former teacher, was a newspaperman in Huron. His early childhood was spent in a sod house on the American frontier. Despite such humble surroundings and because his family so highly prized study and learning, young Herbert was immersed in a world of words. As the Spindens became more affluent they moved into better quarters, and then to Washington State where Herbert attended school and flourished intellectually. After completing public school, he worked for a time as a surveyor, and then went off to Alaska to seek his fortune in the gold rush. As with so many fortune hunters before him, Spinden did not strike it rich, so he quickly got over gold fever and turned again to more scholarly endeavors.

Entering Harvard University in 1902, Spinden eagerly embraced the disciplines of archaeology and anthropology. He returned to the plains to conduct his first excavation in the summer of 1905 at a Mandan site in North Dakota (Spinden and Will 1906). After graduating Harvard in 1906, he stayed on there to pursue graduate work in anthropology, studying both archaeology and ethnography, and working in multiple regions, as was customary at that time. He continued his work in the American West, doing ethnographic studies with the Nez Perce of Idaho and Montana (Spinden 1908), while at the same time developing his interest in the archaeology and history of the Maya.

What was probably his most significant work was done in the Harvard library for his doctoral dissertation, which was completed in 1909 and published in 1913 as *A Study of Maya Art*. It was the very first systematic study of the iconography of Maya writing and remained the only one for decades to come. In it, Spinden was among the first to propose that Maya writing was concerned with historical narration and not just chronology. He catalogued the evolutionary development of the stylistic traits of Maya hieroglyphs, and constructed a framework for analysis that considered both the dates on Maya monuments and the style of depictions they contained. After completing *A Study of Maya Art,* he was said to be able to accurately predict the date of a monument from its style alone. This brilliant study is still considered a landmark in the field.

In 1909, after his dissertation was completed and his degree conferred, Spinden embarked on a career as an assistant curator at the American Museum of Natural History in New York City. He held this post from 1909 until 1921, when he was hired away by the Peabody Museum at his alma mater to become their curator of Mexican archaeology and ethnology. Continuing his ascent in the museum field, he eventually left Harvard to take a position as curator of anthropology at the Buffalo Museum in 1926. His last career move was in 1929 when he joined the prestigious Brooklyn Museum as curator of American Indian art and primitive cultures. He served there until his retirement in 1951. Throughout his professional life, Spinden was a productive scholar, dedicated both to anthropological research and to the public dissemination of knowledge. He was not only active in the field as a researcher and a collector for the museums that employed him, but also as a museum scholar—curating exhibitions, writing, and lecturing.

His next major book was the original 1917 edition of *Ancient Civilizations of Mexico and Central America* (Spinden 1917a). In it, Spinden was reluctant to propose a specific correlation between the modern Gregorian calendar and the Maya Long Count. By 1928, however, when the third edition was published, he had concluded that the calendar correlation problem had been solved, and he proposed a correlation that was widely accepted: i.e., that the year A.D. 1539 corresponded to the Maya Long Count date 12.9.0.0.0. His was one of six or eight possible correlations proposed by the mid-1920s—and was indeed a leading contender—although no one could say with authority which of these was correct. In 1930, the problem was apparently solved when John Teeple published a study of Maya astronomy which suggested that a competing correlation proposed by Goodman, Martinez, and Thompson was more likely to be accurate. The GMT solution differed from Spinden's in offering a correlation that was 260 years later. They placed A.D. 1539 at the Maya Long Count equivalent of 11.16.0.0.0. By the 1950s, early radiocarbon dating turned the tables on this hypothesis and suggested that Spinden's correlation was probably more likely to be right after all. But, in the 60s and 70s, after further refinements in carbon-dating techniques and careful study of documentary and archaeological materials, the GMT correlation was corroborated. Spinden was close, but off the mark by 260 years, or a period of five 52-year cycles.

Spinden's devotion to humanist principles, social justice and racial equality was amply and frequently demonstrated. He worked for the conservation of the nation's heritage by arguing that archaeological sites needed protection against looters and developers who wished to exploit them for personal gain. He battled as a conservationist for the protection of land in the face of rapacious farming practices and industrial exploitation. He militated for better treatment of Native American peoples by the Bureau of Indian Affairs—an organization that often seemed to oppress rather than to uplift the people it was charged to protect. He was an active opponent of the BIA's support of off-reservation Indian schools that consciously sought to deprive Native American children of their tribal identity. He was also dedicated to bringing about a recognition of the inherent value of the lives and works of native peoples whom some scorned as savages (Spinden 1927). In fact, throughout much of his career, he used his expertise in Maya art to uphold the creative genius of Native Americans against the racist views of diffusionists who argued that all the intellectual achievements of the Americas had originated in the Old World, usually in Europe (cf. Spinden 1924a, 1924b). Spinden died in 1967, ten years after completing his last major publication *Maya Art and Civilization*, in which much of his work and ethics were reprised.

Ancient Civilizations of Mexico and Central America

This new edition of *Ancient Civilizations of Mexico and Central America* is not only important as evidence of the value of Spinden's first popular synthesis of Meso-american culture, but also—in the spirit of past as prologue—as a presentation of the shortcomings of the archaeology of his period, and the origins of our knowledge in this area. Spinden was somewhat hampered in having performed his work before the advent of radiocarbon dating, and before there was much adequate archaeological work in his primary areas of interest. He tried to place events in chronological order using an evolutionary seriation of style which worked to a limited extent but was rife with problems. In this context, some of Spinden's erroneous generalizations may be seen to have derived from too limited an evidentiary base.

The book begins with a description of the geography and natural environment of the region, and a cursory history of its discovery and conquest by the Spanish in the early sixteenth century. The first chapter presents a survey of the "Archaic Horizon," a term Spinden uses to refer to the period of early settled village life during which people farmed for a living, and made and used pottery. His "Archaic," now known as the Formative or Preclassic, was a period in which he hypothesized a time of wide cultural integration and innovation—a period when patterns of future cultural evolution were established. Without an accurate chronology or a clear understanding of the process of domestication, he simply lumped domestication in with early ceramic development, thereby condensing a long time span into a short discussion. Indeed, it was not until the 1930s, 1940s and even 1950s that many of the chronological problems that we now see in Spinden's work were settled (cf. Vaillant 1941); but the conception that regional integration both followed from and led to the sharing of important ideas has endured.

Spinden's capacity to describe complex images in evocative terms is nowhere better demonstrated than at the beginning of the second chapter, which covers the civilization of the Maya. His inspiring descriptions of their art and architecture are as eloquent as ever. The discussion of what is known about Maya hieroglyphs is, of course, completely out of date. We now know a great deal more than we did in 1928 (cf. Houston 1993, Schele and Freidel 1990, Schele and Miller 1986, Thompson 1950, 1962, and many, many others). Spinden's discussion of the Maya calendar, though intricate, is as straightforward and comprehensible as any that I have seen, despite the correlation problem. The structure of the calendar is the same after all, whatever the correlation scheme used.

I would note that the Tuxtla Statuette is no longer the earliest dated object. (Using the GMT correction, the date on the Tuxtla Statuette is actually in the year A.D. 162.) That distinction now belongs to Stela 2 from Chiapa de Corzo, with a date that corresponds to December 7, 36 B.C. Other early dates are found at the Olmec site of Tres Zapotes—32 B.C., and the Mixe-Zoquean site of La Mojarra—A.D. 143 and 156. The earliest date from the Maya area proper is thought to be on a monument from the site of El Baúl, probably A.D. 36. Another point that needs correction concerns the invention and elaboration of the Long Count calendar. Spinden thought that the Maya were responsible, but it seems ever more likely that the calendar was developed in the Gulf Coast area well before the Maya began to make use of it.

Spinden's summary of Maya history is 260 years too early throughout. One must only remember that 260 years need to be added to all of the Gregorian equivalents to the Maya Long Count dates to convert to the more accurate GMT correlation. Spinden's periods are defined numerically by the Maya calendar and have limited cultural significance. They are only approximately similar to

the more familiar chronological terms of modern scholar-
ship. The correspondences are, in order: Terminal
Formative (or Preclassic), Early Classic, Late Classic,
Terminal Classic, Early Postclassic, Late Postclassic.
Spinden's last two time periods cross the boundaries of
Late Postclassic and Early Colonial and Later Colonial to
Modern. Spinden's discussion of the cause of the "collapse" of the Classic Maya at the end of what he calls the
"Great Period," now known as the Terminal Classic, is
fanciful and clearly incorrect. Much of his discussion of
the Postclassic periods and the role of Quetzalcoatl and
the Toltec is similarly flawed. The chronology problem is
exacerbated in the Postclassic because his dates were
based on both the Long Count and on highland Mexican
historical accounts. The 260-year correction rule that I
proposed above does not always work here.

Spinden's third chapter focuses on the state of archaeological knowledge with regard to a variety of "middle"
or "lesser civilizations" as of 1928. He used these terms to
refer to everyone except the Maya and the Aztec. Because
of his lack of chronological control, Spinden was unable
to correctly place these cultures in time. He attributes
most of their development to influence from the Maya.
He begins the discussion, for example, with a brief consideration of the Olmec; but he had only the most rudimentary knowledge of the Olmec because in 1928 only
two Olmec sites were known, neither of them well-
known. The La Venta site had been discovered in 1925,
and Spinden himself had discovered the site of Cerro de
las Mesas in 1927. The extent to which he recognized that
the Olmecs pre-dated the Maya is not clear.

His discussion of the other cultures in this section is
similarly—although not quite so drastically—dated.
Modern scholarship on the Zapotec, the Mixtec, the
Totonac, and the Toltec cultures, as well as on sites like
Teotihuacan and the others, should be consulted before
too much stock is placed in Spinden's analysis. This is
nowhere more evident than in the capricious discourse

about Quetzalcoatl and the Toltec, where Spinden's conclusions are generally unsupported by the evidence.

The fourth chapter considers the history and culture of
the Aztecs. Spinden begins by positing an analogy that
compares the Maya and Aztecs in the New World to the
Greeks and Romans in the Old World. In fact, the similarities are nowhere near as great as he imagined,
although the comparison is apt in at least some particu-
lars. The calendric correlation for the Aztec period is
essentially correct because it is based on central Mexican
sources rather than on Spinden's erroneous reconstructed
correlation of the Maya Long Count. Here Spinden also
presents a simple overview of the history and culture of
the Aztec people, drawn from ethnohistoric accounts and
limited archaeological evidence, that is quite readable
and generally reliable. He also describes and interprets
the three most famous carved stone monuments of Aztec
civilization—the Calendar Stone, the Stone of Tizoc, and
the Coatlicue statue—all discovered in the late eighteenth
century. His descriptions of the Aztec religion and a few
of the central deities are fine, but his explanations of the
origin of Quetzalcoatl and Xipe Totec are not generally
accepted.

Spinden concludes the book with an important theoretical proposition about the development of culture history
in the New World. He proposed, first in a 1917 article
(Spinden 1917b) and then in a more elaborate form in this
edition of *Ancient Civilizations of Mexico and Central
America,* that cultural evolution in the New World was
progressive, spreading through space and developing
through time. He postulated that the development of
more complex societies throughout the Americas began
with the emergence of agriculture, pottery, and loom
weaving in Central Mexico during the "Archaic" period.
This process began with the domestication of a variety of
food plants in the arid highlands, and the subsequent
invention of pottery. Progress ensued as these same
domesticated plants became adapted to life in the more

humid lowlands, while other lowland plants were being domesticated as well. Spinden believed that these developments led ultimately to the emergence of civilization and the recording of history. He carefully examined the evidence then available and noted shared patterns of development replicated in many parts of the New World, from the Arctic to the tip of South America. Hence his theory that cultural development evolved by means of the diffusion of ideas from a common tradition rooted in the archaic highlands of Mexico.

Ancient Civilizations of Mexico and Central America ends with a chart that embodies this regional and evolutionary hypothesis. Putting aside the fact that the "Archaic" was not the simple, localized period of emerging innovation and subsequent smooth expansion that he envisioned, Spinden's developmental hypothesis set scholarship on the right road for years to come. Many shared characteristics of cultures did indeed coalesce during the Formative period (Spinden's "Archaic"); and the complex societies of both Middle and South America were ultimately built upon the base of productive agriculture.

Herbert Joseph Spinden was a remarkable scholar. His work is important. It is not unassailable, it is not flawless, but it is important. He fought for social justice for Native American people long before it was fashionable to do so. We owe him a debt for the work that he did and the work that he stimulated in the generations of archaeologists, anthropologists, ethnohistorians, art historians, and museologists who have followed.

Bruce E. Byland

New York
1999

REFERENCES CITED

Beyer, H.
  1918   *Apuntas Acerca de un Nuovo Manual de Arqueología Mexicana.* Mexico.

Brunhouse, R. L.
  1975   *Pursuit of the Ancient Maya: Some Archaeologists of Yesterday.* University of New Mexico Press, Albuquerque.

Houston, S. D.
  1993   *Hieroglyphs and History at Dos Pilas: Dynastic Politics of the Classic Maya.* University of Texas Press, Austin.

Joyce, T. A.
  1914   *Mexican Archaeology: An Introduction to the Archaeology of the Mexican and Maya Civilizations of pre-Spanish America.* New York and London, 1914.

Lumholtz, C.
  1902   *Unknown Mexico,* 2 vols. New York.

Morley, S. G.
  1915   *An Introduction to the Study of Maya Hieroglyphs.* Smithsonian Institution, Bureau of American Ethnology, Bulletin 57. Washington, D.C.

Peñafiel, A.
  1890   *Monumentos del Arte Mexicano Antiguo: Ornamentación, Mitología, Tributos y Monumentos,* 3 vols. Berlin.

Prescott, W. H.
    1843   *History of the Conquest of Mexico,* 3 vols. London.

Schele, L. and D. Freidel
    1990   *A Forest of Kings: The Untold Story of the Ancient Maya.* William Morrow, New York.

Schele, L. and M. E. Miller
    1986   *The Blood of Kings: Dynasty and Ritual in Maya Art.* George Braziller, New York, in association with the Kimbell Art Museum, Fort Worth, Texas.

Seler, E.
    1902–8   *Gesammelte Abhandlungen zur Amerikanischen Sprach- und Alterhumskunde,* 3 vols. Berlin.

Spinden, H. J.
    1908   "The Nez Perce Indians." American Anthropological Association Memoirs 2, pt. 3:165–274.

    1913   *A Study of Maya Art: Its Subject-Matter and Historical Development.* Memoirs of the Peabody Museum of Archaeology and Ethnology, Harvard University, vol. 6. Cambridge, MA.

    1917a   *Ancient Civilizations of Mexico and Central America.* American Museum of Natural History, Handbook Series no. 3, New York.

    1917b   "The Origin and Distribution of Agriculture." 19th International Congress of Americanists 1915, pp. 269–76, Washington, D.C.

1924a   "What about the Indian?" World's Work 47: 381–84.

1924b   "Letter from Dr. Herbert J. Spinden . . ." Eastern Association on Indian Affairs. Bul. 3:12–14.

1927   "Can civilized man keep savage virtues?" Forum 78:346–56.

1957   *Maya Art and Civilization,* revised and enlarged. Falcon's Wing Press, Indian Hills, Colorado.

Spinden, H. J. and G. F. Will
    1906   "The Mandans: A Study of Their Culture, Archaeology, and Language." Peabody Museum Papers 3, no. 4, pp. 81–319.

Stephens, J. L.
    1841   *Incidents of Travel in Central America, Chiapas, and Yucatan,* 2 vols. New York.

Teeple, J.
    1930   *Maya Astronomy.* Carnegie Institution of Washington, publication 403, Contribution 2. Washington, D.C.

Thompson, J. E. S.
    1950   *Maya Hieroglyphic Writing: An Introduction.* Carnegie Institution of Washington, publication 589. Washington, D.C.

    1962   *A Catalog of Maya Hieroglyphics.* University of Oklahoma Press, Norman.

Vaillant, G. C.
    1941   *Aztecs of Mexico.* Garden City.

Wauchope, R.
   1965   *They Found the Buried Cities: Exploration
            and Excavation in the American Tropics.*
            University of Chicago Press, Chicago.

Willey, G. R. and J. A. Sabloff
   1974   *A History of American Archaeology.* W. H.
            Freeman, San Francisco.

PREFACE

THIS little book is intended as a general commentary and explanation of the more important phases of the ancient life and arts of the Indians of Mexico and Central America, and especially of their history. The substance of it is drawn from many sources, for the anthropologist must mould together and harmonize the gross results of several sciences. Archæology, ethnology, somatology, and linguistics all make their special contributions and we are only on the threshold of our subject. In the Mexican and Central American field we find the accumulated writings that result from four hundred years of European contact with the Indians and in addition a mass of native documents and monumental inscriptions expressed in several hieroglyphic systems.

The general method of this book will be to take up in order the recognized "horizons" of pre-Columbian history, beginning with the earliest of which we have knowledge. In relation to each horizon we will examine the records and discuss the principal developments in arts, beliefs, and social structures. The introductory chapter is designed to put before the reader such facts as may be necessary for a ready understanding of the discussions and explanations that will follow.

The Mexican Hall of the American Museum of Natural History furnishes illustrations of most of the facts given herewith. This Hall contains both originals and casts brought together by various expeditions of the Museum and of other scientific institutions. The principal patrons of science whose names should be mentioned in connection with the upbuilding of these collections are: Willard Brown, Austin Corbin, R. P. Doremus, Anson W. Hard, Archer M. Huntington, Morris K. Jesup, James H. Jones, Minor C. Keith, the Duke of Loubat, William Mack, Henry Marquand, Doctor William Pepper, A. D. Straus, I. McI. Strong, Cornelius Vanderbilt, Henry Villard, William C. Whitney. But thanks are also due to innumerable persons who have contributed single specimens and small collections as well as those who have placed information at the disposal of the scientific staff. The principal collectors have been: George Byron Gordon, Aleš Hrdlička, Carl Lumholtz, Francis C. Nicholas, Marshall H. Saville, Eduard Seler, Herbert J. Spinden, and John L. Stephens.

CONTENTS

MAPS AND ILLUSTRATIONS

INTRODUCTION

Geography and Natural Environment. Unfortunately the terms "Mexico and Central America" are not mutually exclusive. Central America is a natural division comprised between the Isthmus of Tehuantepec and the Isthmus of Panama. Mexico is a political division that includes several states in Central America, namely, Chiapas, T a b a s c o , Campeche, Yucatan, and the territory of Quintana Roo. The ancient high cultures of Mexico hardly extended as far north as the Tropic of Cancer and the region beyond this is of slight interest to us. P o s i t i o n s south of Mexico will often be referred to the areas of the modern political units although these have no immediate relation to pre-Spanish conditions. These political units are: Guatemala, British Honduras, Honduras, Salvador, Nicaragua, and Costa Rica.

Fig. 1. The Great Snowstorm of 1447 shown in the Pictographic Record of the Aztecs called Codex Telleriano Remensis.

Although lying within the tropics, the territory extending from the Isthmus of Panama to Central Mexico exhibits great extremes of climate and topography and hence of plant and animal life. The year is everywhere divided into a wet and a dry season but the relative duration of each depends upon land form and altitude. The coast of the Pacific is considerably drier than that of the At-

13

lantic. Three climatic zones are generally recognized, namely, the *Tierra Caliente* (Hot Land), *Tierra Templada* (Temperate Land), and *Tierra Fria* (Cold Land), and in some regions each of these has an arid and a humid strip. The change from luxuriant forests to open thorny deserts is often very sudden. On the high plateau or *Tierra Fria* the natural warmth of the latitude is largely overcome by the altitude. In the Valley of Mexico snow falls only at rare intervals, yet chilling winds are common in the winter. Much of the plateau from Mexico south into Guatemala is open farming land well suited to the raising of maize and wheat where water is sufficient. The shoulders of the mountains bear forests of pine and oak while the highest peaks are crowned with perpetual snow.

A description of the mountains, rivers, and lakes will help towards an understanding of the problems that are before us. The broad plateau, crossed by irregular ranges of mountains, that occupies the states of New Mexico and Arizona continues far south into Mexico. On the western rim the Sierra Madre lifts a great pine-covered barrier, beyond which the land drops off quickly into the hot fringe of coastal plain bordering the Pacific Ocean and the Gulf of California. The highest mountains of the western Sierra Madre are El Nevado and Colima, the first a snowy peak 14,370 feet high and the second an active volcano 12,278 feet high. On the eastern rim of the central plateau the second Sierra Madre is less continuous but it culminates in the loftiest peak of all Mexico—the wonderful cone of Orizaba. This mountain rises from the tropical jungles well into the region of perpetual snow and attains an elevation of 18,314 feet above the sea.

[a]

[b]

Plate I. (a) Village Scene in Arid Mexico. Cactus and other thorny shrubs are ever present. The houses of the natives are of adobe with thatched roofs. (b) In the Humid Lowlands. The view shows part of the plaza at Quirigua with one of the monuments almost concealed in vegetation of a few months' growth.

15

Its name in Aztecan is Citlaltepetl, which means Star Mountain. Two other famous peaks of Mexico are Popocatepetl and Iztaccihuatl, both names being pure Aztecan. The first means Smoking Mountain and the second White Woman. These volcanic crests rise into the snowy zone from the table-land which is itself about 8,000 feet above the sea.

In southern Mexico the plateau area enclosed between the principal sierras narrows perceptibly,

Fig. 2. The Smoke reaches the Stars, a Mexican Picture of a Volcanic Eruption in the Codex Telleriano Remensis.

because the shore line of the Pacific and the mountain range that parallels it swing more and more towards the east. At the Isthmus of Tehuantepec a low valley separates the highland area of Mexico from that of Central America. This second table-land is not so wide as the one we have just considered and is more deeply dissected by rivers. The mountains of Guatemala rise to a considerable altitude, the highest being Tacaná with 13,976 feet elevation. Active volcanoes are numerous and earthquakes frequent and often disastrous. The Volcan de Agua and the Volcan de Fuego (Volcano of Water and Volcano of Fire) look down upon Cuidad Vieja and Antigua Guatemala, the old Spanish capitals which each in turn destroyed. The cordillera still presents its most abrupt front to the Pacific and on the eastern side, in Guatemala and Honduras, there are high forest-bearing ridges between the river systems. The Cockscomb Mountains in British Honduras are a low outlying group. In southern Nicaragua the main chain is broken by a low broad valley that extends from ocean to ocean. In Costa Rica and Panama a single range stretches midway along the narrow strip of land, with peaks that rise above 11,000 feet.

The lowland strip on the Pacific side of our area is a narrow fringe. Like the central plateau it is for the most part arid, but irrigation makes it productive. The lowlands of the Atlantic side are generally wet and heavily forested. The greatest land mass of uniformly low elevation is the Peninsula of Yucatan. In eastern Honduras and Nicaragua there are extensive river valleys of low elevation.

The river systems of Mexico and Central America flow into the two bounding oceans or into lakes which have no outlets. Several closed basins occur on the Mexican table-land. The Rio Nazas and the Rio Nieves flow into salt marshes in the northern state of Coahuila. But the most important interior basin is the Valley of Mexico. In this mountain enclosed valley, whose general level is 7,500 feet above the sea, there are five lakes which in order from north to south are named Tzompanco, Xaltocan, Texcoco, Xochimilco, and Chalco. The last two contain fresh water, since they drain into Lake Texcoco, but the rest are more or less brackish. Lake Texcoco is by far the largest, although its area has been greatly reduced by natural and artificial causes since the coming of the Spaniards.

The largest river of Mexico is the Rio Lerma which takes the name Rio de Santiago during its deep and tortuous passage from Lake Chapala to the Pacific. Farther to the south is the Rio de las Balsas which likewise flows into the western ocean. The name means "River of the Rafts" and is given because of a peculiar floating apparatus made of gourds tied to a wooden framework that is used on this stream. Flowing into the Gulf of Mexico are several large streams, among which may be mentioned the Panuco, Papaloapan, Grijalva, and Usumacinta. The last is by far the greatest in volume of water, and with its maze of tributaries drains a large area of swamp and jungle in which are buried some of the most wonderful ruined cities of the New World.

In the northern part of Yucatan there are no rivers on the surface on account of the porous limestone. Instead there are great natural wells called *cenotes* where the roofs of subterranean rivers have fallen in. Many of the ancient cities were built near such natural wells.

Passing to the south the most important river of Guatemala is the Motagua, which has cut a fine valley through a region of lofty mountains. In Honduras there are several large rivers, including the Uloa, Patuca, and Segovia. The lake region of Nicaragua is drained by the San Juan River that flows into the Caribbean Sea. Nearly all the streams of Central America that flow into the Pacific are short and steep torrents. An important exception is the Lempa River that forms part of the interior boundary of Salvador.

Concerning lakes, mention has already been made of Chapala and Texcoco, the most important in Mexico. The former is about fifty miles in length. In the state of Michoacan there are a number of beautiful lakes intimately connected with the history and mythology of the Tarascan Indians. The most famous is called Patzcuaro. In southern Yucatan the shallow body of water known as Lake Peten also has a distinct historical interest. Several lakes in Guatemala are well known on account of the rare beauty of their situation. Lake Atitlan is surrounded by lofty mountains, and Lake Izabal, or Golfo Dulce, is famous for the luxuriance of the vegetation that screens its banks. Lakes Nicaragua and Managua are well known on account of their connection with the much-discussed canal projects. The Island of Ometepe in Lake Nicaragua bears an active volcano.

In regard to the geology it is only necessary to point out a few of the more important characters. The highlands which bear so many active and quiescent volcanoes naturally show great masses of eruptive rocks, some due to recent action and others much more ancient. Porous tufa is a common material for sculptures in many parts of Mexico and Central America. In other places there are great beds of softer and finer grained material also of volcanic origin. In these places, such as Copan in western Honduras and Mitla in southern Mexico, building in stone received its greatest development. The soft greenish stone of Copan seems to be a solidified mud flow permeated with volcanic ash rather than a true lava flow of melted rock. Limestones are also common and important in the economic development. In some regions there are beds of a hard, blue limestone going back to the Carboniferous epoch. This stone makes an excellent cement after burning. The Peninsula of Yucatan is a great plain of limestone of much more recent formation. Like our own Florida it was once a coral reef which was lifted above the sea by some natural agency. This limestone gets older and more solid as we approach the base of the peninsula but at best is rather porous and coarse-grained.

The fauna and flora present great variation. In the moist lowlands the monkeys play in the tree tops and the jaguar lies in wait for its prey. Alligators and crocodiles infest the rivers and swamps. Two small species of deer and the ocellated turkey are important items in the meat supply of Yucatan, that includes also the iguana, the peccary, and various large rodents. The tapir and manatee are the largest animals of the lowlands but neither seems to have been of great significance to

Fig. 3. Yucatan Deer caught in a Snare. From the Mayan Codex, Tro-Cortesianus.

the natives. Bats are frequently represented in the ancient art and a bat demon appears in several myths.

Upon the highlands of Mexico the Toltecan deer is still hunted, together with the wild turkey that is the parent of our domestic birds. The turkey was, in fact, domesticated by the Mexican tribes. It probably occurred southward over the Guatemalan highlands, but is now extinct in this latter region. In the southern part of Central America the

Fig. 4. The Moan Bird, or Yucatan Owl, personified as a Demigod. Dresden Codex.

place of the turkey as an item of diet is taken by the curassow, a yellow-crested bird with black plumage. The coppery-tailed trogon, the famous quetzal, was sacred in ancient times and is now the emblem of Guatemala. This beautiful bird occurs only in the cloud cap forest zone on the high mountains of southern Mexico and Guatemala. Blue macaws, parrots, paroquets, and humming birds contributed their gay plumage to adorn headdresses and feather-covered cloaks. These and many other birds doubtless flitted about in the aviary of Moctezuma. The black vulture, the king vulture, and the harpy eagle are other conspicuous birds often figured in the ancient art. The coyote, ocelot, and puma are the principal beasts of prey on the highlands.

Among the characteristic trees of the lowlands may be mentioned the palm, which occurs in great variety, the amate and ceiba, both of which attain to large size, as well as mahogany, Spanish cedar (which is not a cedar at all but a close relative of the mahogany), campeche, or logwood, rosewood, sapodilla, and other trees of commerce. Upon the higher mountain slopes are forests of long-leaf pine and of oak. In the desert stretches the cactus is often tree-like and there are many shrubs that in the brief spring become masses of highly-colored blossoms.

Some of the principal crops of Mexico and Central America have been introduced from the Old World, including coffee, sugar cane, and bananas. Other crops such as maize, beans, chili peppers, cocoa, etc., are indigenous. Among the native fruits may be mentioned the aguacate, or alligator pear, the mamey, the anona, or custard apple, the guanabina, jocote, and nance.

History of European Contact. The great area with which we are concerned has been in touch with Europe since the beginning of the sixteenth century. Columbus, on his last voyage in 1502, landed on the northern coast of Honduras and rounded the stormy cape called Gracias à Dios. Later he skirted the shore of Costa Rica and Panama and entered the body of water which was named in his honor Bahia del Almirante—Bay of the Admiral. He brought back sensational news of the gold in possession of the natives, which they had told him came from a district called Veragua. After a few years of stormy warfare the Spaniards established themselves firmly in this golden land. Vasco Nuñez de Balboa, who emerged from the bickering mob as the strongest leader, was the first white man to cross the Isthmus. This he did in 1513, grandiloquently laying claim to the Pacific Ocean and all the shores that it touched in the name of Spain. The crown appointed the greedy and black-hearted Pedrarias Davila governor of Darien and in 1517 he succeeded in having Balboa beheaded on a flimsy charge. Colonization and exploration went forward rapidly. In 1519 the old city of Panama, now in ruins, was founded. The rich region around the Nicaraguan lakes was discovered by Gil Gonzalez Davila and the city of Granada was founded in 1524. The exploration from the southern base came in contact with that from the north in Salvador shortly after this event.

Fig. 5. Spanish Ship in the Aubin Codex.

Let us now direct our attention to the conquest of

[a]

[b]

Plate II. (a) Site of Pueblo Viejo, the First Capital of Guatemala; (b) A Spanish Church at the Village of Camotan on the Road to Copan.

23

Mexico. Perhaps the Portuguese were the first to sight the mainland of Yucatan in 1493. There is little to prove this except one or two charts or maps made in the first decade of the sixteenth century that show the peninsula in its proper location. In 1511 or 1512 a ship from Darien was wrecked and some of the sailors were cast upon the coast of Yucatan. Most of them were killed and sacrificed, but two survived. One of these survivors was Geronimo de Aguilar, who later was rescued by Cortez and became his guide and interpreter.

The first accredited voyage of discovery to Mexico was one under the command of Francisco Hernandez de Cordoba, which sailed from Cuba in February, 1517. He coasted the northern and eastern shores of Yucatan. When he attempted to obtain water he was worsted in a serious battle with the Maya Indians. His expedition finally returned to Cuba in a sad plight. The next year Juan de Grijalva set out to continue the exploration of the new land with the stone-built cities. He landed at Cozumel Island and took possession. He explored the eastern coast of Yucatan as well as the northern and western ones, discovered the mouth of the large river that bears his name, and proceeded as far as the Island of Sacrifices in the harbor of Vera Cruz.

The next year Hernando Cortez was sent out by Velasquez, the governor of Cuba, to conquer the new land. He landed at Cozumel Island and rescued Geronimo de Aguilar. Then he followed the coast to the mouth of the Grijalva River where he disembarked and fought the important battle of Cintla, the first engagement in the New World in which cavalry was used. After a signal victory Cortez continued his way to Vera Cruz. Here delay and dissension seemed about to break the luck of the invaders.

Although the Mexicans were somewhat inclined to regard the Spaniards as supernatural visitants and to associate their coming with the fabled return of Quetzalcoatl, the Plumed Serpent, still Mocte-zuma refused to grant an interview to Cortez. The Totonacan city of Cempoalan opened its gates and became allies of the invaders. Final-ly, at the instigation of their stout-hearted cap-tain, the Spaniards de-stroyed their ships on the shore in order to steel t h e i r resolution through the impossibil-

Fig. 6. Cortez arrives with Sword and Cross and Mocte-zuma brings him Gold. Codex Vaticanus 3738.

ity of retreat. Then the little band of 450 white men with their retinue of natives marched towards the highlands. The route led past Jalapa and over the mountains to the fortified city of Tlaxcala. This city, after a skirmish, likewise enlisted in the Span-ish cause, a course that came easy because Tlaxcala was a traditional enemy of Tenochtitlan, the ancient Mexico City, and had withstood the attacks of the Aztecs for many years. From here Cortez passed to the sacred city of Cholula where, suspecting treachery, he caused many of the inhabitants to be massacred.

In the Spanish histories one hears much con-cerning the omens, the prophecies, and the vain appeals to the gods that became more and more frequent and frantic as the invaders approached

the capital. Arriving at Ixtapalapan they entered
upon the great causeway leading out to the Venice-
like city in the lake. Accepting the inevitable,
Moctezuma and his nobles met the Spaniards and
conducted them to the Palace of Axayacatl, which
was prepared for their habitation. This took place
in November, 1519. The fears of Moctezuma were
soon fulfilled, for he was taken prisoner and held as
a hostage of safety in his own capital.

Fig. 7.   Aztecan Canoe.   Lienzo de Tlaxcala.

Meanwhile Velasquez, convinced of the unfaith-
fulness of Cortez, dispatched Narvaez to capture the
rebellious agent. But Narvaez was himself captured and his soldiers went to augment the army
of the victor.

Alvarado had been left in command of the gar-
rison at Tenochtitlan during the absence of Cortez.
The time approached for the great feast of Tezcatlipoca and the Spaniards, fearing the results of
this appeal to the principal Aztecan god, resolved
to be the first to strike. The multitude assembled

in the temple enclosure was massacred and after this deed the soldiers fought their way back to the stronghold in which they were quartered. The Aztecs were thoroughly aroused by this unwarranted cruelty as well as by the cupidity of the Spaniards. Cortez hastened back to take personal charge; but in spite of victories in the storming of the pyramids and in other hand-to-hand contests, the invaders were so weakened that their condition was truly alarming. Moctezuma died in captivity and the last restraint of the natives was removed.

The night of June 30, 1520, is famous as La Noche Triste—The Sad Night—for on this night the Spaniards attempted to steal out of the city that had become untenable. The natives were warned by a woman's shriek and a desperate encounter took place on the narrow causeway leading to Tlacopan. The bridges were torn down and the Spanish soldiers in armor were hemmed in between the deep canals. At last, however, the firm land was reached. Here, instead of following up the victory, the natives permitted the Spaniards to re-form their ranks. A few days later Cortez was able to restore something of his lost prestige by the decisive victory at Otumba, after which he continued his retreat to the friendly Tlaxcala.

A year was spent in recuperation, in building boats for an attack from the lake, and in putting down the Aztecan outposts. In the meantime the natives were suffering from a dreadful visitation of smallpox, introduced by the Spaniards, and Cuitlahuac, the successor of Moctezuma, had died of this disease after a rule of eighty days. Finally Tenochtitlan was besieged again. The buildings were leveled to the ground as the Spaniards advanced.

[a]

[b]

Plate III. (a) View of the Island Town of Flores in Lake Peten where the Last Capital of the Itzas was located; (b) The Sacred *Cenote* at Chichen Itza into which Human Beings were thrown as Sacrifices, along with Objects of Jade and Gold.

The brave defense of Cuauhtemoc availed for naught against cannon and steel armor. On the 13th of August, 1521, the conquest of Tenochtitlan was achieved and the spirit of a warlike people forever broken.

The Valley of Mexico having been taken, numerous expeditions were sent out to subdue the more distant provinces and to establish colonies. Alvarado invaded the south and by 1524 he had captured Utatlan and other native strongholds on the highlands of Guatemala and had invaded Salvador. Cortez himself undertook a wonderful march from Vera Cruz to the Gulf of Honduras to punish an unruly subordinate. His course lay through the swamps and jungles of the Usumacinta Basin, thence across the savannahs of southern Yucatan to Lake Peten, and, finally, over the mountains to Lake Izabal and the Motagua River. Even today much of his route would be called impassable for an army. Puerto Cortez, on the northern coast of Honduras, was founded at the conclusion of this expedition. The exploitation of Yucatan and Tabasco was granted to Francisco Montejo, who began the conquest of this low-lying territory in 1527. The first campaigns were disastrous and heartbreaking. Several short-lived Salamancas were founded, one of them at Chichen Itza. But the odds were too great and by 1535 all the Spaniards had been killed or expelled. The son of Montejo renewed the struggle. In 1540 Campeche was founded and early in 1542 the city of Mérida was established upon the site of an earlier Mayan town.

Progress was also rapid in the north. Nuño de Guzman departed in 1529 on a mission to conquer Michoacan and the great northern province known

as New Galicia. His rule was marred by many acts
of cruelty. In 1538 Coronado, the successor of
Guzman, led his army northward to the land of the
Pueblo Indians and then out into the Great Plains.
Before the first English settlement was made in
North America the power of Spain was firmly estab-
lished, not only throughout Central America and
Mexico, but also in the southwestern part of the
United States.

The spiritual conquest was no less remarkable
than the territorial. The priests accompanied and
even preceded the armies with the doctrine of the
cross. The rough and ready characters that enliven the wonderful drama of this period had the
vices of greed and cruelty, but nearly all were
imbued with a pride of religion, if not with the true
flame. The firmness and bigotry on the one hand
and the open sympathy on the other with which the
Catholic fathers met the practical problems before
them resulted in vast achievements. Either by acci-
dent or design certain patron saints and efficacious
shrines of special interest to the natives were not
long in becoming known. The Virgin of Guadeloupe
and the Black Christ of Esquipulas brought many
converts to the foreign faith. Church building was
carried on apace. The various religious orders became rich and powerful and exerted a strong influence upon civil administration.

The later history of this great region can be
passed over briefly. Cortez was the first governor
general of Mexico but he was soon shorn of his
power as dictator at large. The First Audiencia
was appointed in 1528 and is noteworthy simply by
reason of its misrule. The Second Audiencia, beginning two years later, put through some excellent

reform laws. The first Viceroy, the great and good Mendoza, arrived in 1535 and for fifteen years the land prospered under his rule, which was benign without being weak. He was succeeded by Luis de Velasco, who emancipated many of the enslaved Indians. The long line of viceroys continued until 1821, when Spain was forced to relinquish her provinces in America. Among the greatest of the viceroys was Bucareli, the forty-sixth in line, who ruled Mexico from 1771–1779 while the United States of America were just beginning to feel the pulse of life.

During the viceregal period in Mexico the region to the south was ruled by the captain general of Guatemala. The dominion was subdivided into five departments corresponding to the modern republics of Guatemala (which then included the Mexican state of Chiapas), Honduras, Salvador, Nicaragua, and Costa Rica. Panama was ruled from the South American province of New Granada.

Weakened by Napoleonic wars and rent by internal dissensions, Spain found herself in the first two decades of the nineteenth century unable to maintain her waning power in America. Bolivar and his brother patriots raised the standard of revolt in South America in 1810 and in the same year war for independence broke out in the north. Hidalgo, the parish priest of Dolores, rang the liberty bell of Mexican freedom on the 16th of September, 1810. This beloved patriot was captured the year following, and shot, but the revolution, once begun, was continued under Morelos and other leaders. After 1815 the cause seemed hopeless, but in 1820 there was a new uprising and General Iturbide, who was sent to put it down, turned his army against the

government and established himself as emperor.
Central America was also included in this Mexican
empire. The rule of Iturbide soon became unpopu-
lar and in 1823 he abdicated his throne. The Mexican republic that was then instituted continued until
the French intervention in 1861. During this time
the most noteworthy events were the war with the
United States in 1846–47 and the passing of the
reform laws under Benito Juarez that freed Mexico
from the oppressions of the church.

As a result of the French intervention Maximilian
of Austria was made emperor. This unfortunate
ruler, who did much to beautify Mexico City, was
dethroned and shot in 1867. The republic was then
re-established.

The other republics of Central America formed a
federal union at the time the first Mexican empire
came to an end in 1823. This union was preserved
till 1839 and several later attempts were made to
restore it. The five republics have had such tem-
pestuous careers as a result of warfare, usurpation,
and political brigandage that their material and social development has been stunted. Several are
now, however, on the high road to stability.

Panama was until 1903 a part of Colombia. British Honduras had its origin in the concessions given
to English logwood gatherers and to the fact that
pirates found refuge behind the coral reefs that line
the shores. The English claim to the Mosquito
Coast rested upon a similar flimsy basis, and was
finally abandoned.

Languages. The twenty distinct stocks of related
languages formerly recognized in Mexico and Central America have now been greatly reduced. Of

those that remain, some occupied small areas and had little in the way of dialectic variation, while others stretched over wide territories and were divided into many mutually unintelligible tongues, which, in turn, were subdivided into well-defined dialects. Several stocks are now approaching extinction through the substitution of Spanish. A number of languages, however, are still spoken by hundreds of thousands of natives.

The language having the greatest geographical extension within the area under consideration is the Mexican, or Nahuan, now consolidated with the Piman, Shoshonean, etc., in a great stock called the Uto-Aztecan. In its extent this stock may be compared to the Indo-Iranian of the Old World which comprises most of the modern and ancient languages of Europe as well as those of a large part of Asia. Within the United States are the numerous Shoshonean tribes found as far north as Idaho, reaching into California on the one hand and into Texas on the other. In southern Arizona and northwestern Mexico come the Piman group. East of the Sierra Madre are the Tarahumare and the Tepehuano. These languages are mutually unintelligible, although morphologically related, and all are subdivided into dialects. The relationship is proved through laborious comparison and analysis of the words and grammar, in the same way as the philologist proves that Persian, Greek, Russian, English and Welsh are all cognate tongues. Farther to the south are still other divisions of the stock; including the Huichol and Cora of the mountainous region north of Guadalajara and the Mexican or Aztecan of the Valley of Mexico and adjacent country. The Mexican language is still spoken by a million or more natives and is divided into a number of dialects. Properly the Aztecs are a single tribe whose chief city was Tenochtitlan, the ancient Mexican City. They first appear on the page of history as the Mexitin, along with the closely related Chalca, Xochimilca, etc. The people of Central Mexico called their language Nahuatl, meaning "clear speech" and nicknamed their relatives to the south, Pipil, or "boys" because they spoke awkwardly. Mexican colonies were widespread before the coming of the Spaniards and during the Conquest the distribution of this nation was made still greater. The Mexicans, and especially the natives of Tlaxcala, accompanied the Spaniards on military expeditions against other tribes and as a consequence many place names in southern Mexico and Guatemala were translated into their language. There were, however, large groups of Indians of Mexican stock already located in southern Guatemala and in Salvador. Still farther south were the Niquirao of Nicaragua and a little-known group called the Sigua in Costa Rica.

The wide geographical distribution of Uto-Aztecan languages has an undeniable historical significance. The numerous tribes represent a very wide range in culture albeit nearly all are dwellers of arid or semi-arid regions. Some like the Paiute, are miserable "diggers" willing to eat anything that will support life; others like the Comanche are warlike raiders; more progressive tribes like the Hopi have adopted agriculture and developed interesting arts and customs; while the highest members of the group are among the most civilized nations of the New World. It seems clear that language can be used as a basis of classification

over a much greater stretch of time than can other
social habits summed up as "culture." Particular
phases of art, religion, and government develop and
disappear, but the grouping of sounds used to express ideas remains as proof that peoples now far
apart geographically, as well as in their habits and
achievements, were once close together. The peculiar distribution of the Uto-Aztecan languages
may indicate a general southward movement of the
stock.

The second most important linguistic stock is the
Mayan, now spoken by over half a million people.
This stock has only one outlying member, namely,
the Huasteca of northern Vera Cruz. The other
twenty-one languages cover a continuous area in the
Mexican states of Yucatan, Tabasco, and Chiapas,
and in the republic of Guatemala. The most important language of the group is the Maya proper,
which is spoken by the natives of Yucatan and by
the Lacandone Indians of the Usumacinta Valley.
The Tzental, Quiché, Cakchiquel, Chol, and Chorti
are other prominent languages.

In the region of the Isthmus of Tehuantepec are
the Zapotecan and Mixtecan stocks, which differ
widely in sound and structure from the Mayan and
Nahuan tongues that hem them in. West and east
of the Valley of Mexico are, respectively, the Tarascan and Totonacan stocks, which show no great
amount of subdivision. In Honduras, Nicaragua,
and Costa Rica are several language groups that
have never been carefully studied. It seems likely
that some of these will be consolidated when words
and grammatical structures are better known. The
Chiapanecan languages were spoken in three localities on the Pacific side of Nicaragua and Costa Rica,

while a fourth division occupied a small area far to the northwest on the banks of the Chiapas River. It is now believed that the Otomi group, as well as a number of minor languages, including the Mazatecan, belong in a single stock with the Chiapanecan. If this supposed connection should prove true a northern movement of the stock would be pretty surely indicated. Several members of the Subtiaban stock show the same south to north movement and here there is evidence that the migration took place some three centuries before the coming of the Spaniards. Parts of the Isthmian region were held by tribes having linguistic affiliation with South America and it is not unlikely that a considerable back flow from South America made itself felt along the Atlantic coast of Central America, if we may judge by ethnological features and by suggested linguistic connections.

The great Hokan stock has now been extended from California across northern Mexico to Texas, taking in the Seri and numerous other tribes of low culture. For the most part these tribes are extinct or at least have lost the ancient speech.

Ethnology. To a less extent than the native languages the old-time customs still hold out against the tide of European influence. In regions not easily accessible on account of deserts, mountains, or tropical jungles, there are a number of Indian tribes that preserve in a large measure their ancient arts and ideas. But the study of these remnant peoples has not been very thorough.

The Pima, Seri, Tarahumare, Tepehuane, and other tribes of the extreme north and northwest of Mexico have until recent times been comparatively unmodified by Spanish influences. Basketry, textiles, and pottery have been maintained by them as well as many religious ceremonies. Farther south among the Cora and Huichol there also are surviving arts. The woven fabrics of these Indians are

Fig. 8. Design on Modern Huichol Ribbon.

Fig. 9. Woven Pouch of the Huichol Indians showing Two-Headed Austrian Eagle.

very beautiful but introduced ideas are frequently seen. For instance, a very common motive in Huichol textile art is the two-headed Austrian eagle evidently taken from the coins of Charles V. Crowns similar to those worn by the two-headed eagle are often shown on the heads of rampant animals. But most of the motives are doubtless of native origin.

Among the Huichol and Tarahumare the curious *peyote,* or *hikule* worship may be studied. A small variety of cactus is eaten, which induces ecstasy or stupor accompanied by color visions and peculiar dreams. Elaborate ceremonies are associated with the eating and gathering of this plant. The religious cult of the peyote has swept over a large portion of the Great Plains Area of the United States and is known even to Indians in the neighborhood of the Great Lakes. There can be no doubt that the narcotic action of the peyote was known to the Aztecs, who made a ceremonial use of it under the name *teonanacatl.* An intoxicating drink called *teswin* is commonly made in northern Mexico from the heart of the mescal plant. It takes the place of the famous *pulque,* the ancient beverage of the Mexican highlands. Hunting dances in which are employed regalia and ceremonial objects of great interest occur among the Huichol and neighboring tribes. The so-called "god's eyes" made of yarn strung spider-web fashion over crossed sticks are practically identical with the "squash blossoms" of the Pueblo Indians. There are also real temple structures, or "god houses," which are very significant when we consider the former importance of the temple among the more highly civilized peoples to the south. In these and other respects the Huichol culture is about midway between the culture of the Southwestern Pueblo tribes and that which formerly existed in central Mexico.

Elsewhere in northern and central Mexico it is possible to find many suggestions of ancient Indian ways of living. In nearly all the outlying villages

the old-time thatched huts are still used, while
baskets, gourd vessels, wooden bowls, earthen pots,
and other household objects hark back to native origins, although often modified by European contact.
For instance, glazing is commonly seen on the modern pottery. Many travelers in Mexico bring away
as souvenirs pieces of pottery from Guadalajara
and Cuernavaca. These wares are made by Indians, but in decoration they have only slight traces
of the ancient art of the Mexicans.

In dress there are noteworthy survivals. The
serape made either on the narrow hand loom or on
a crude form of the Spanish tread loom is a pic-
turesque element in the national dress that is
rapidly disappearing from view. Time was when
the rich plantation owner wore a gayly colored
blanket on *fiesta* days. The most famous centers
for the manufacture and sale of blankets were the
cities of Saltillo and San Miguel. The Saltillo pattern shows a medallion consisting of concentric dia-
monds in various colors upon an all-over design in
stripes. The motives are minute geometric figures
skilfully interlocked. The colors are rich and permanent and are combined in a very pleasing manner.
Saltillo blankets must be classed among the finest
textile products of the world. The best period was
before 1850. San Miguel blankets show characteristically a rosette instead of a diamond in the center.
Many beautiful blankets come from other localities
in Mexico. The Chimayo blankets have the same
part Indian, part Spanish origin and are made by
the Spanish-speaking natives in the mountain valleys of New Mexico.

In southern Mexico there are many towns of
Indians where the women still wear the finely em-
broidered huipili. This old-time garment varies

[a]

[b]

Plate IV. (a) A Guatemalan *huipili* decorated with Highly
Conventionalized Animals in Embroidery; (b) Pouches of the
Valiente Indians of the Chiriqui Lagoon, Panama.

40

considerably in different towns but as a rule it is a simple sack-like gown cut square at the neck and with short sleeves. Sometimes it is shortened to a blouse, and is worn with a skirt; at other times a short huipili is worn over a longer one. An easily visited town where the natives still wear the old-time dress is Amatlan, within an hour's walk of Cordova. The women of the Isthmus of Tehuantepec have a gorgeous costume of which the most remarkable feature is a wide ruff worn around the neck or on the back of the head. The Mayan women of Yucatan wear white huipili with needlework in color around the bottom. On the highlands of Guatemala the huipili is usually a blouse. The skirt sometimes consists of a strip of cloth wrapped several times around the body.

An interesting ceremony which survives in some parts of Mexico and Guatemala has as its principal feature a lofty pole with a swivel arrangement at the top to which long ropes are attached. These ropes are wound round the swivel and performers, who may be dressed like birds, attach themselves to the rope ends. During the process of unwinding the performers whirl dizzily around the pole descending lower and lower and swing in a wider and wider circle till they reach the ground.

The Lacandone Indians live in the marshy jungles that border the winding Usumacinta. They speak the same tongue as the Maya Indians of Yucatan but in the matter of culture they have acquired little from the Spaniards. They still weave simple garments and make pottery vessels. In hunting they use the bow and arrow, the latter usually tipped with a point of stone. In their religious practices they use incense burners which are comparable to those of the sixteenth century.

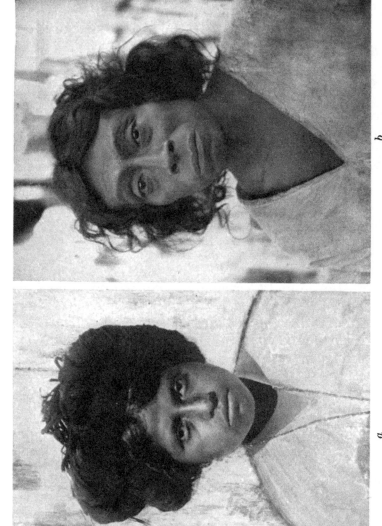

a

b

Plate V. (*a*) Zapotecan Girl from the State of Oaxaca, wearing a Turban-Like Headdress made of Yarn; (*b*) Lacandone Man from Southern Mexico. Wavy hair is sometimes seen among the few members of this Mayan tribe.

The Caribs occupy the greater part of the north coast of Guatemala and Honduras, running east from the port of Livingston on the Gulf of Amatique. These people, originally of South America and later of the West Indies as well, were deported by the English from the Island of St. Vincent in 1796. They have now established themselves in the new land where they raise the manioc or cassava root and press out the poisonous juice in a basketry tube as do their kindred in the Orinoco Valley. Long before the forcible immigration it is likely that the Caribs, who were cannibalistic in habit, had raided the shores of Central America in their seagoing canoes. A significant passage in the chronicles of the Mayas states that naked man-eating savages visited Yucatan long before the coming of the Spaniards.

The Mosquito Indians of the east coast of Nicaragua and Honduras have a very considerable negro admixture. They are fishermen of low culture. Farther inland are found the Sumo who flatten the heads of their children and who hold strange feasts in honor of the dead in which the dancers are masked so that none may be recognized. A string is stretched over the tree tops from the grave to the feasting place and over this string the ghost of the dead person is supposed to walk. When everyone has fallen in a drunken stupor from *mishla* the ghost of the dead man departs for the land of the dead. These Sumo Indians build large houses with open sides and are very skilful at fishing with bow and arrow and steering their canoes through white rapids. They practise polygamous marriages, weave cotton, and make interesting beadwork ornaments.

In the narrow Isthmian region there are tribes of

Indians that resist manfully the inroads of civilization. Perhaps the best known of these are the San
Blas Indians who inhabit the mountain fastnesses
east of the Canal Zone. In northern Costa Rica the
Guatuso and Talamanca tribes still maintain to a
considerable degree their old native character.

Physical Types. Minor physical differences in
stature, head form, and facial expression mark off
pretty clearly the tribes of this area from each other.
The stature is lowest among the Mayas and Maza-
tecs, the average being about 5 feet 1 inch, while
among the Tarascans, Tlaxcalas, and Zapotecs, it
averages about 5 feet 3 inches. The other tribes of
Central America and of central Mexico fall between
these extremes. In northern Mexico the stature
increases considerably, average measurements for
the Yaqui being in excess of 5 feet 6 inches. To
make up for their lack of height the southern Indians are sturdy and heavy muscled, with deep
chests. Their hair is usually black and straight,
but occasionally wavy. Light beards and mustaches
are sometimes worn, especially by the Mayas. The
eyes are so dark brown as to appear black to the
casual observer. They are set rather wide apart
and while usually horizontal they seem, in some instances, to have a slight Mongoloid tilt. Noses vary
greatly but are often finely aquiline. The cephalic
index (obtained by dividing the breadth of the head
by its length and multiplying the result by 100) is
rather high. The Mayas are strongly round-headed
with an index of 85.0 while their linguistic relatives,
the Tzendals, have a medium index of 76.8. The
other tribes of southern Mexico fall between these
extremes. No long-headed peoples are found in
this area although in northern Mexico some tribes
approach the long-headed type.

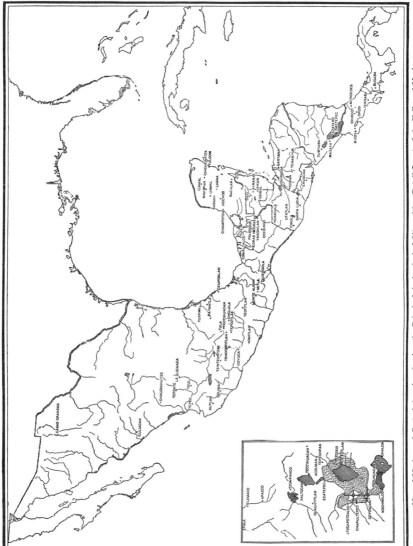

Map of Mexico and Central America showing the Principal Archaeological Sites with a Detail Insert of the Valley of Mexico.

Chapter I

THE ARCHAIC HORIZON

IN 1910 an actual stratification of human products was found in the environs of Mexico City in which three principal culture horizons could be readily discerned. A collection made at the time, illustrating the objects characteristic of the three strata, is on exhibition in the American Museum of Natural History. In parts this stratification verified theories of culture succession already held by students working in this field. Since that time careful research in several localities has been carried on and many authentic specimens from the three layers have been brought together.

The stratigraphic series concerns sedentary life after the invention of agriculture. Presumably a nomadic horizon preceded that of the first farmers, but few traces of this have so far been reported from southern Mexico and Central America. The earliest known specimens of the lowest level are not rudimentary but are well stylized, and opinions vary as to the length of time necessary for a theoretical formative stage. It seems necessary to consider this old civilization as a stratigraphic unit admitting the probability that true beginnings await the archæologist's spade.

The culture of the lowest stratum is here called archaic, a word meaning old, but not necessarily primitive. The word "horizon" carries an implication of chronological succession, but it would not be wise to insist that archaic remains everywhere represent a dead chronological level. Archaic art is oldest in its place of origin, the highlands of Mexico and Central America, and in or near this general region, it was first succeeded by higher types. On the margin of its distribution archaic art, or at least the most striking traits of archaic art, lasted into much more recent times, and in some places may even have survived till the coming of the Spaniards. Even when every allowance is made for independent expressions which may find nearly the same form, it seems that remarkable homogeneity and continuity can be demonstrated for products of the archaic civilization of the New World.

Most of the evidence of the old civilization consists of ceramic objects, but there is also some stonework including implements, ornaments, and crude statues. Common household pottery shows local variations, but as a rule the archaic wares can be recognized as such by qualities of paste, shape, and decoration. The motives are simply geometric or realistic and there is a lack of formalized designs. One process of decoration has wide distribution and seems to have been invented well along in the archaic period. This is the process of negative painting in which the lines of the decorative pattern, originally applied in wax or pitch, stand out in the natural surface color of the pot against an overpainted background. This "batik" pottery extends from central Mexico to northern Peru.

The most interesting and important objects of archaic art in clay are human figurines executed in peculiar styles. These not only reflect details of dress, etc., but also seem to stand for a set of religious ideas. Especially a type of figurine representing a nude female appears to be an agricultural fetish, symbolizing the fecundity of Mother-Earth.

Stratification of Remains. Atzcapotzalco was once an important center of the Tepanecan tribe situated on the shores of lake Texcoco. It was an early rival of Tenochtitlan, the Aztecan capital, and was conquered and partly destroyed in 1439. The principal modern industry of Atzcapotzalco is brick-making, and several mounds and much of the surface of the plain have been removed for this purpose. In the mounds are found many pottery objects of the late Toltecan period, while on the surface of the ground are encountered fragments of the typical Aztecan pottery in use when the Spaniards arrived.

Fig. 10. Atzcapotzalco Destroyed. The temple burns at the Place of the Ant

The stratification of the plain varies in different places so far as the thickness of the different strata is concerned, but the order is always the same. At one locality it is as shown in Fig. 11. First comes a layer of fine soil of volcanic ash origin, probably deposited by the wind. This is five or six feet in thickness, yellowish at the top, and much darker towards the bottom, with streaks and discolorations. The Aztecan pottery is found close to the surface, while Toltecan pottery occurs in the middle and lower sections. Underneath the soil layers lies a thick stratum of water-bearing gravel mixed with sand. This gravel stratum is possibly the old bed of a stream that formerly entered Lake Texcoco near this point. In some places it is fifteen or eighteen feet in thickness. Scattered throughout the gravel are heavy, waterworn fragments of pots as well as more or less complete figurines of the archaic type.

At other sites, such as Colhuacan, the Toltecan
layer is of greater thickness and the archaic layer
of lesser thickness. The remains extend below the
present level of the water and may indicate that

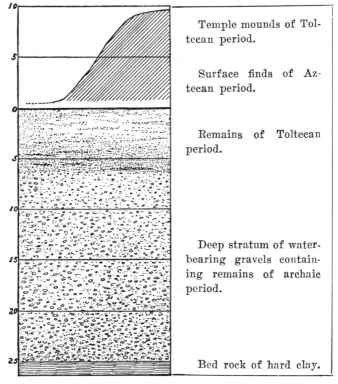

Temple mounds of Tol-
tecan period.

Surface finds of Az-
tecan period.

Remains of Toltecan
period.

Deep stratum of water-
bearing gravels contain-
ing remains of archaic
period.

Bed rock of hard clay.

Fig. 11.   Diagram of Culture Strata at Atzcapotzalco.

considerable changes have taken place in the level
of the lake. But we must remember that many of
the ancient settlements were built over the water
and that land was made in ancient times, as it is
today in the gardens of Xochimilco, by deepening
canals. Archaic remains are also common on the

denuded tops of hills which may once have been covered by soil.

A stratification of archæological remains has recently been determined in Salvador.

The Cemetery under the Lava. An ancient cemetery lying under lava has recently been explored in Copilco, a suburb of Mexico City. The lava swept down from Mount Ajusco in some cataclysm perhaps 3000 years ago, covering many square miles of territory to the depth of thirty or forty feet, and burying such villages as chanced to lie in its path. (See Pl. VI*b*). The discovery of human remains was made several hundred feet back from the original front of the lava flow in a quarry where lava rock was being removed to build roads. Tales of clay figurines found under the lava in this quarry had been current for years, but no serious investigation was made until human burials were met with in the earth under the great lava cap. Then a series of tunnels was dug and a considerable number of ancient burials were uncovered, but not moved from their original position. One now enters an electric-lighted graveyard and sees human bodies lying exactly as they have lain for untold centuries, with the funeral offerings beside them. This enormously important find gives us an historical level in mid-Archaic.

Another site, at Cuicuilco, on the opposite side of the lava flow, has received attention from archæologists. Here a great round mound rises in terraces faced with cobblestones. It is surrounded by the lava flow and some persons have assumed that the mound was already abandoned and in decay when the lava flow took place. Perhaps, however, the

[a]

[b]

Plate VI. (a) Cuicuilco. A view showing cobblestone facing of mound and lava in contact with apron or causeway; (b) Archaic Site under Lava Flow near Mexico City. A local museum has been established at this site in electric-lighted tunnels.

mound was built on a piece of land that the lava flow
had spared. There are no contacts between the lava
and the mound except at the ends of two projecting
aprons or causeways. The pottery at this site is
sufficiently different from that found at Copilco.

Invention of Agriculture. Before examining in
greater detail the art of the Archaic Horizon let us
consider its real signifi-
cance. It is generally
admitted that America
was originally populated
from Asia, but on a cul-
ture level no higher than
the Neolithic. The sim-
ple arts of stone chip-
ping, basketry, fire-mak-
ing, etc., were probably
brought over by the ear-
liest immigrants, b u t
there is abundant evi-
dence that pottery-mak-
ing, weaving, and agriculture were independently
invented long after the
original settlement. The

Fig. 12. *Teocentli* or Mexican Fodder Grass.

cultivated plants in the New World are different
from those of the Old World and there is a vast area
in northwestern America and northeastern Asia,
upon the only open line of communication, where
agriculture and the higher arts have never been
practised.

Now the invention of agriculture is an antecedent
necessity for all the high cultures of the New World.
It is equally clear that this invention must have

taken place in a locality where some important food plant grew in a wild state. By far the most important food plant of the New World is maize. While this plant has changed greatly under domestication, botanists are inclined to find its nearest relative and possible progenitor in a wild grass growing on the highlands of Mexico and known by the Aztecan name *teocentli,* which means sacred maize. It is known that maize is at its best in a semi-arid tropical environment. It cannot be brought to withstand frost although the growing season can be cut down to meet the requirements of a short summer. Geographically its use extended from the St. Lawrence to the Rio de la Plata and from sea level to an elevation of fifteen thousand feet in tropical regions. The Mexican highlands occupy the central position in the area of its distribution and archæological evidence strongly points to this region as being the cradle of agriculture and the attendant arts. Besides maize, the most widely distributed food plants of the New World are beans and squashes. Certain other plants were cultivated in more restricted areas and may have had different places of origin. For instance, manioc was doubtless brought under cultivation in a humid lowland region, probably the Amazon Valley, and the same may be said of sweet potatoes. The common potato was found under domestication in Peru and there is no very good evidence that its use extended into Central America.

Irrigation would have been necessary before agriculture could have been developed to any great extent on the highlands of Mexico. Although irrigation is often looked upon as a remarkable sequel of the introduction of agriculture into an arid country, yet from the best historical evidence at our command we should rather regard it as a conception which accounts for the very origin of agriculture itself. The earliest records of cultivated plants are from Mesopotamia, Egypt, Mexico, and Peru where irrigation was practised. In these regions are also seen the earliest developments of the characteristic arts of sedentary peoples, namely, pottery and weaving, and the elaborate social and religious structures that result from a sure food supply and a reasonable amount of leisure.

If this theory is true we must admit that below the Archaic Horizon we should find traces of a horizon of non-agricultural peoples, living a nomadic life without pottery. Unfortunately, such peoples make fewer objects and scatter them more widely than do sedentary agriculturists.

No one on the basis of present knowledge can offer more than an opinion concerning the date of the invention of agriculture in the New World. The thick deposits left by the sedentary peoples argue great age and the wide area of homogeneous products argues slow change. In the most favored regions archaic art may have been succeeded by higher forms shortly before the time of Christ, and perhaps 5000 years is not too long a time to allow for the diversities of the domesticated plants of America.

Archaic Figurines. Archaic art is characterized by figures of men and women modeled in clay and sometimes painted. The forms are peculiar and the technique well standardized. Most are modeled in a flat gingerbread fashion into a gross shape. Upon this gross shape special features are indicated by

Plate VII. Large Archaic Figures found in Graves and offering Evidence of Ancient Customs and Arts and also showing a Quality of Caricature or possibly Portraiture. These are probably late products since they come from Tepic and Jalisco, where archaic art maintained itself long after its disappearance from central Mexico.

stuck-on ribbons and buttons of clay and by gougings and incisings with some pointed instrument.

Fig. 13. Archaic Figurines from Central Mexico. The first three specimens are from under the lava at Copilco.

Fig. 14. Archaic Figurines—Zapotlan, Jalisco; Tampico, Vera Cruz; and Cuesta Blanca, Salvador.

Modeling was done entirely by hand, moulds being as yet unknown. The figurines are usually from two to five inches in height and often represent nude women in sitting or standing positions with the hands upon the knees, hips, or breasts. The heads are characteristically of slight depth compared with their height, the limbs taper rapidly from a rather plump torso and hands and feet are mere knobs with incised details. When the figures are intended to stand erect, as is often the case, the feet show signs of having been pinched between the thumb and fin-

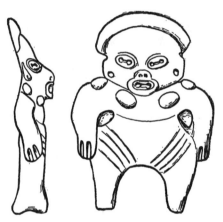

Fig. 15.   Archaic Figurine from Salvador.

ger of the potter so that they have a forward and backward cusp and a broad base of support. Groovings are seen in connection with the hair, eyes, mouth, fingers, toes, and details of dress and ornament. Paint is often added to this surface to indicate tattooing, textile patterns, etc.

The eyes of the archaic images—and the mouths as well—are made according to several methods. First, there is the simple groove; second, a groove across an applied ball or button of clay; third, a round gouging made by the end of a blunt implement held vertically; fourth, a round gouging in an applied ball or button of clay; fifth, two gougings made with a round or chisel-edged implement held at an angle. The second form of eye, which resembles a grain of coffee, and the fifth form with the double gouging made from the center outward, are found from the northern limits of archaic art in Mexico as far south as Colombia and Venezuela.

Fig. 16.   Types of Eyes of Archaic Figurines.

The technique of manufacture naturally changes somewhat with the increase in size. There is also reason to believe that the largest hollow figures come from the end of the Archaic Period in Mexico, and especially those that have been found in the state of Jalisco and the territory of Tepic. The eyelids are often rather carefully modeled and sometimes an eyeball is put in between the lids. These and perforated eyes seem to be the latest characters to be developed in the archaic art and it is significant that they are not found over such a wide area as the first five types of eyes given above.

Ancient Customs. We may gather much of an ethnological nature from the study of these quaint figures. Articles of dress and adornment are shown as well as musical instruments, weapons, etc. Headdresses may consist of fillets, turbans, and objects perched on one side of the head. Noserings and earrings are abundantly represented and in considerable variety. We may be sure that weaving was rather highly developed because many garments

such as shirts, skirts, and aprons are painted or
incised with geometric designs. Body painting, or
tattooing, appears to have been a common usage.
Among weapons the *atlatl,* or spear-thrower, was
already known and knobby clubs seem to have been
popular. Men are shown beating on drums and
turtle shells, while women nurse children and carry
water. Since the large figures of clay are often

Fig. 17. Textile Designs painted on Archaic Effigies.

found in tombs it is not impossible that they were
intended to be portraits of the dead. Many have a
startling quality of caricature.

Archaic art is a pretty certain index of the religion then in vogue. There is a notable absence of
purposely grotesque or compounded figures representing divinities such as will be found in the later
horizons. We miss entirely the characteristic Mexican gods such as Tlaloc and Ehecatl. Dogs are
frequently modeled in clay and were apparently

developed into a rather special domestic breed. Snakes are sometimes found as a plastic decoration on pottery but there are few signs of serpent worship. We can find no evidence that human sacrifice was practised. The presence of human figurines in graves has already been mentioned and the suggestion made that some of them may have been intended as portraits of the dead. Nude female figurines in sitting or standing positions have an unbroken distribution from Mexico into South America and it is not unlikely that the primitive agriculturists associated them with fertility and used them as amulets to secure good crops. The male figurines may have been votive offerings for success at arms.

Archaic Pottery. The ordinary pottery of the Archaic Period from Mexico and Central America is heavy and simple in shape. The globular bowl

Fig. 18. Typical Tripod Vessels of the Archaic Period, from Morelos, Mexico.

with a constricted neck is a common form as well as wide-mouthed bowls with or without tripod supports. Lugs and handles are very common. When plain, the tripods are large, hollow and rounded, with a perforation on the under side, but they are often modified into faces and feet. Many vessels are decorated by the addition of modeled faces enabling us to make a direct connection with the figures in clay already described.

In fact the decoration of pottery of this early pe-

[a]

[b]

Plate VIII. Two Stages in the Stone Sculptures of Costa Rica. Note that in the first series (a) the human body is adapted to the surface of a boulder with the arms, legs, and face in low relief and with eyes, nose, and mouth all protruding, while in the second series (b) the limbs are rounded and partly freed from the body. Both are of archaic type but probably not of great age.

60

riod is predominantly in relief. Paint is sparingly used and then only in the simplest geometric fashion. There is a general lack of conventionalized motives presenting animals and other natural forms in highly modified ways. In later ages the painted decoration is much concerned with the serpent, but except for a few winding serpents in relief, this motive is not seen on the pottery of the Archaic Period.

Stone Sculptures of the Archaic Period. The earliest stone sculptures are recognized first by resemblance to the ceramic art just described and second by a quality which they possess of being archaic in an absolute sense. The greater difficulty of working

Fig. 19. Series showing the Modification of a Celt into a Stone Amulet. State of Guerrero, Mexico, probably late Archaic.

stone as compared with clay and the longer time required in the process makes stone art less subject to caprice than ceramic art. Perhaps the most primitive examples of stone sculpture are boulders rudely carved in a semblance of the human form with features either sunken or in relief. The arms and legs are ordinarily flexed so that the elbows

[a]

[b]

Plate IX. (a) Stone Sculptures of the Archaic Period. This resembles the pottery as regards style: the eyes protrude and the limbs are carved in low relief against the body; (b) Typical Site of the Archaic Period. The use of pyramids may have begun towards the end of this period.

meet over the knees. The eyes and mouths in the most carefully finished pieces protrude, but the face has little or no modeling. Many celts are modified into figures by grooves, and faces are frequently represented on roughly conical or disk-shaped stones.

We know very little from actual excavations concerning houses of the Archaic Period. It is likely that they were small and impermanent, possibly resembling the modern huts. The pyramidal mound as a foundation for the temple may have been developed towards the end of the Archaic Period. It would be interesting to determine whether adobe moulded into bricks was known at this time, as it was at a later time in the same region, or whether walls were built up out of fresh mud possibly reinforced by slabs of stone.

Extensions of the Archaic Horizon. The curious objects of ceramic art that we have found deeply buried under the débris of higher civilizations in the Valley of Mexico can be traced far and wide. They are encountered, for the most part, in arid and open country, and since we have every reason to believe that the earliest agriculture was developed under irrigation, it is but natural to find the use of agriculture spreading first into other arid regions. And if there was an association between the fertility of Mother-Earth and little fetishes representing women then these fetishes would spread as part of the agricultural complex.

It now seems possible that the cult of the female figurine reached our Southwestern states on the earliest level of agricultural life. In sites belonging

to Basket-Maker III—the archæological level of the
first Pueblo pottery—little female fetishes are found
and, indeed, are symptomatic of this early culture.
They are cruder than anything as yet found in Mexico, but not necessarily older. With them occurs a
primitive maize doubtless introduced from the south.

In the Isthmian region, on the other side of the
Mexican and Central American cradle of New World
agricultural civilization, there are small figurines
quite similar to the archaic figurines of Mexico and
Salvador as regards pose and bodily proportions.
These are mostly on the level of the first Mayan
civilization even in cases where the coffee-grain eye
is used. Around the Nicaraguan lakes the figurines
of nude females were cast in moulds, a device entirely unknown on the Archaic Horizon in Mexico.
In the Nicoya Peninsula of Costa Rica the figurines
are skilfully modeled with painted designs in black
on a dark brilliant red, which may represent tattooing. In the Chiriqui Province of Panama the figurines belong in a ceramic group characterized by
the use of highly conventionalized alligators or
crocodiles. It has already been stated that designs
of the Archaic Horizon in Mexico are either geometric or naïvely realistic. There is another matter
that deserves attention: some of these southern
types of the female fetish occur in distinctly humid
lands and this, by itself, is a strong argument
against great antiquity.

The Isthmian female fetish must have been implanted on the Archaic Horizon even though the
present examples are mostly from post-archaic
times. Perhaps future archæological investigation
will reveal early stations of a purely archaic type in

Plate X. Widely Distributed Female Figurines: (a) Nicaragua; (b) Panama; (c) Venezuela; (d) Island of Marajo, Brazil.

65

desert parts of Costa Rica and Panama. Till then a controlling fact is that Mayan religious art avoids all references to sex and cannot, therefore, possibly be held responsible for the culture trait of the female fetish. But this fetish does agree with a pre-Mayan concept, as we have seen.

The ancient gold work of Costa Rica and Panama also reflects the technique of archaic art, although most of it, to judge by the religious significance of many of the subjects and designs, was made long after the Archaic Period. Just as the pottery figurines were built up by the addition of ribbons and buttons of clay to a generalized form so the patterns for gold castings were made by adding details in rolled wax or resin to a simple underlying form of the same material.

In Colombia and Venezuela archaic art is common in arid and mountainous territory. Local developments confuse the issue of time. Various cultural successions took place here, the Quimbaya, Sinu, and Tairona Indians having developed civilizations with possible Mayan affiliations in some features. The archaic figurines of Colombia are decorated with designs made by the process of negative painting through the medium of wax. This process is pretty generally distributed from central Mexico to northern Peru. The indications are that it was invented long before the rise of the Mayas, and once invented remained popular.

As regards Venezuela the figurines of men and women from the Eastern Andes are often strikingly similar to those of Mexico, especially in such matters as eyes made by double gougings. As a rule, these figurines are painted. Around Lake Valencia they are made without paint, but in combination with pottery designs showing the beginnings of conventionalization. Here there is added the circumstance that wild Carib tribes, coming down the Orinoco, drove the earlier inhabitants out over the West Indies. This flight must have taken place centuries before the coming of the Spaniards.

The archæology of the lower Amazon is best known from the remains found on the Island of Marajo where female figurines exhibit close similarity in pose to specimens from Venezuela and Mexico. This culture of Marajo seems to have been disrupted before the coming of Europeans. But it may be significant that crude fetishes representing women are used at the present time by tribes on the margins of the old Amazonian culture area. The earliest level at Ancon, Peru, yields ware recalling northern products. Nude females, apparently of somewhat later time, however, are in standing rather than sitting pose. It seems, then, that the trail of dissemination of agriculture and the ancillary arts can be followed across the northern part of South America and southward along the Andes to Peru. The greatest similarities must be sought in the oldest objects and some leeway granted in the case of marginal survivals.

It is proper to speak of agriculture, pottery-making, and weaving as the great civilizing complex. Few inventions could break down the ordinary boundaries of language and environment, as these had done. Yet, after the discovery of America, the horse, introduced by the Spaniards, spread rapidly through native tribes, modifying their lives greatly. It is capable of demonstration that with the horse went two types of saddle—the pack saddle and the riding saddle. Similarly in the first rapid spread of agriculture went pots and woven garments.

Two maps of the New World are given herewith: the first showing the extent of the Archaic Horizon and the second the final distribution of pottery among the American Indians and the final distribution of agriculture. The agricultural area is subdivided according to, first, the arid land type where irrigation is generally practised; second, the humid land type; and third, the temperate land type. The first type of agriculture appears to be the earliest and the range coincides, for the most part, with the range of the archaic pottery art.

Summary. In concluding this section let us sum up the general facts of ancient American history as these appear in relation to the archæological evidences of the Archaic Horizon.

I. Pre-Archaic Horizon

The peopling of the New World from Asia by tribes on the nomadic plane of culture.

II. The Archaic Horizon

Invention and primary dissemination of agriculture, together with pottery-making and loom-weaving. Homogeneous culture with undeveloped religion and unsymbolic art adjusted to arid tropics.

III. Post-Archaic Horizon

Specialized cultures in North, Central, and South America dependent upon agriculture. Strong local developments in esthetic arts, re-

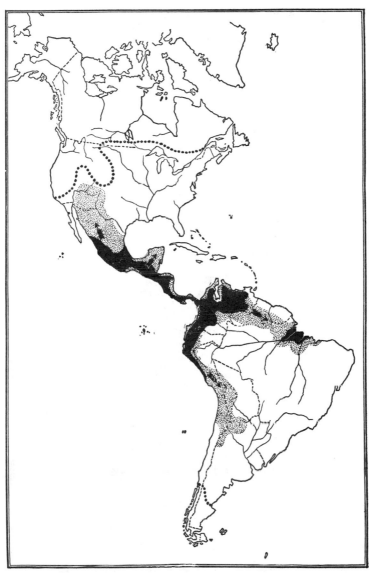

Plate XI. Distribution of the Archaic Culture. The areas in solid black show the distribution of figurines of the archaic type; the areas in dots show the probable extension of pottery on the Archaic Horizon; the dotted lines give the ultimate extension of pottery.

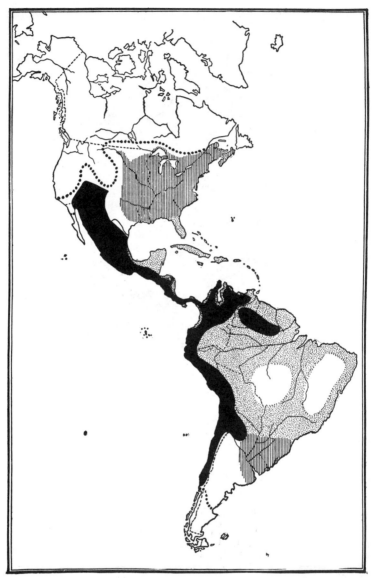

Plate XII. Distribution of Agriculture in the New World.
The dotted line gives the limits of pottery; solid black, agriculture
in arid regions of considerable altitude, mostly with irrigation;
dotted areas, agriculture under humid lowland conditions; lined
area, agriculture under temperate conditions.

70

ligious ideas, and social institutions. Agriculture extended to humid tropical and temperate regions.

We will now make an effort to analyze still further the historical levels in the Post-Archaic Horizon.

Plate XIII. A General View of the Ceremonial Center of Copan. After a model and drawing by Maudslay. The artificial acropolis with temples on pyramids and with sunken courts is in the foreground and beyond is seen the Great Plaza in which monuments are set up. The Copan River has cut into the side of the acropolis and made a natural cross-section.

CHAPTER II

THE MAYAN CIVILIZATION

THE wonderful culture of the Mayan Indians to which we will now turn our attention was developed in the humid lowlands of Central America and especially in the Yucatan Peninsula. Artists are everywhere of the opinion that the sculptures and other products of the Mayas deserve to rank among the highest art products of the world, and astronomers are amazed at the progress made by this people in the measuring of time by the observed movements of the heavenly bodies. Moreover, they invented a remarkable system of hieroglyphic writing by which they were able to record facts and events and they built great cities of stone that attest a degree of wealth and splendor beyond anything seen elsewhere in the New World.

The Mayan culture was made possible by the agricultural conquest of the rich lowlands where the exuberance of nature can only be held in check by organized effort. On the highlands the preparation of the land is comparatively easy, owing to scanty natural vegetation and a control vested in irrigation. On the lowlands, however, great trees have to be felled and fast-growing bushes kept down by untiring energy. But when nature is truly tamed she returns recompense many fold to the daring farmer. Moreover, there is reason to believe that the removal of the forest cover over large areas affects favorably the conditions of life which under a canopy of leaves are hard indeed.

The principal crops of the Mayas were probably

[a]

[b]

Plate XIV. (a) View of the Plaza at Copan from the North-western Corner. This view shows the monuments in position and the steps which may have served as seats; (b) View Across the Artificial Acropolis at Copan. A sunken court is shown and the bases of two temple structures of the Sixth Century. Photographs by Peabody Museum Expedition.

74

much the same as on the highlands, with maize as the great staple. Varieties favorable to a humid environment had doubtless been developed from the highland stock by selective breeding as agriculture worked its way down into the lowlands. Archaic art appears along the edges of the Mayan Area in the state of Vera Cruz, Mexico, and in the Uloa Valley, Honduras. In both these regions are also found clay figurines that mark the transition in style between the archaic and the Mayan, as well as finished examples of the latter. There can be no doubt, then, that the archaic art of Mexico marks an earlier horizon than the Mayan. Whether or not it was once laid entirely across the Mayan Area cannot be decided on present data but it seems unlikely. We have already seen that this first art was distributed primarily across arid and open territory.

With their calendarial system already in working order the Mayas appear on the threshold of history 600 years before the Christian Era, according to a correlation with European chronology that will be explained later. The first great cities were Tikal in northern Guatemala and Copan in western Honduras, both of which had a long and glorious existence. Many others sprang into prominence at a somewhat later date; for example, Palenque, Yaxchilan or Menché, Piedras Negras, Seibal, Naranjo, and Quirigua. The most brilliant period was from 300 to 600 A. D., after which all these cities appear to have been abandoned to the forest that soon closed over them. The population moved to northern Yucatan, where it no longer reacted strongly upon the other nations of Central America and where it enjoyed a second period of brilliancy several hundred years later.

[a]

[b]

Plate XV. (a) Model of the Temple of the Cross, Palenque, designed to show the Construction. The building has three entrances separated by piers. The middle partition is thickened to support the weight of the roof comb which is a trellis for stucco decoration. The sanctuary is a miniature temple in the inner chamber. The walls are built of slabs of limestone set in lime cement; (b) Detail of Frieze on the Temple of the Cross. The upper band is the sky with stars and planets. A reptilian monster occupies the main panel with human figures as supplementary decorations upon his legs. The Temple of the Cross represents the highest achievement of the First Empire architects, Fifth Century after Christ.

Architecture. The idea of a civic center is admirably illustrated in Mayan cities, particularly those of the first brilliant period. The principal structures are built around courts or plazas and there is usually an artificial acropolis which is a great terraced mound serving as a common base or

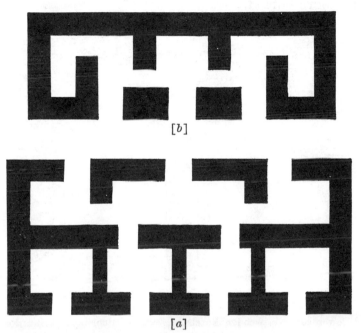

Fig. 20. Groundplans of Yaxchilan Temples: (*a*) Structure 42; (*b*) Structure 23.

platform from which the individual pyramidal bases of several temples rise. At some sites this acropolis is a natural hill which has been trimmed down or added to, but at other sites it is entirely artificial. At Copan there is an especially fine example of artificial platform mound rising from one end of the Great Plaza and affording space for several temples, as well as for sunken courts with stepped sides that may have been theatres. The river washing against one side of this great mound has removed perhaps a third of it and made a vertical section that shows the method of construction. It is apparent that the mound was enlarged and old walls and floors buried.

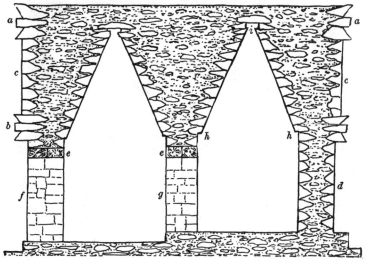

Fig. 21. Cross-section of Typical Mayan Temple in Northern Yucatan: *a*, upper cornice; *b*, medial cornice; *c*, upper zone; *d*, lower zone; *e*, wooden lintels; *f*, exterior doorway; *g*, interior doorway; *h*, offset at spring of vault; *i*, cap stone.

Mayan buildings are of two principal kinds. One is a temple pure and simple and the other has been called a palace. The temple is a rectangular structure crowning a rather high pyramid that rises in several steps or terraces. As a rule the temple has a single front with one or more doorways and is approached by a broad stairway. The pyramid is ordinarily a solid mass of rubble and earth faced with cement or cut stone and rarely contains compartments. Some temples have but a single chamber while others have two or more chambers, the central or innermost one being specially developed into a sanctuary. The so-called palaces are clusters of rooms on low and often irregular platforms. These palaces may have been habitations of the priests and nobility. The common people doubtless lived in palm-thatched huts similar to those used to-day in the same region.

The typical Mayan construction is a faced concrete. The limestone, which abounds in nearly all parts of the Mayan Area, was burned into lime. This was then slaked to make mortar and applied to a mass of broken limestone. The facing stones were smoothed on the outside and left rough hewn and pointed on the inside. It is likely that these facing stones were held in place between forms and the lime, mortar, and rubble filled in between. The resulting wall was essentially monolithic. The rooms of Mayan buildings are characteristically vaulted but the roof is not a true arch with a keystone. The vault, like the walls, is a solid mass of concrete that grips the cut stone veneer and that must have been held in place by a false work form while it was hardening. The so-called corbelled arch of overstepping stones was doubtless known to the Mayan builders but was little used. Taking the single rectangular room as the unit of construction the width was limited to the span of the vault, which seldom exceeded twelve feet, while the length was indeterminate.

The first variation from the temple with one rectangular room was the two-roomed structure with one chamber directly behind the other. In

Plate XVI. A Temple at Hochob showing Elaborate Façade Decorations in Stucco. Probably ninth century. The design over the door represents a grotesque front view face of which the eyes can still be plainly made out. At either side of the door the design represents a serpent head in profile. Photograph by Maler.

this case there were two vaulted compartments separated from each other by a common supporting wall pierced by one or more doorways. The inner room was naturally more dimly lighted than the other one and as a result was modified into a sanctuary, or holy of holies, enhanced by sculptures and paintings, while the outer room developed gradually into a portico. The outer wall was cut by doorways till only pier-like sections remained, and finally these piers were replaced by square or round columns. The development of the Mayan temple may be traced through a thousand years of change and adjustment.

Much attention was paid by Mayan builders to the question of stability which was accomplished directly by keeping the center of gravity of the principal masses within the supporting walls rather than by the use of binding stones. The cross-section of a two-roomed temple of late date will illustrate how this was done. There are three principal masses, one over the front wall, one over the medial partition, and one over the back wall. The roof where these sections join is of no great thickness. The central mass is symmetrical and, if the mortar has the proper cohesiveness, very stable. For the front and back masses the projection of the upper or frieze zone tends to counterbalance the overhang of half the vault. In the earlier temples the upper zone of the façade often slopes backward so that the balance is not so perfect.

So far we have given brief space to the question of elevations. Taken vertically there are three parts to the Mayan building: first, the substructure or pyramidal base; second, the structure proper; third, the superstructure. In the case of temples

Plate XVII. A Sealed Portal Vault in the House of the Governor at Uxmal, a Building of the Second Empire, probably Thirteenth Century. The veneer character of the cut stone comes out clearly. Peabody Museum photograph.

the structure proper is one story in height. Two and three stories are rather common in palaces, but the upper stories are in most cases built directly over a solid core and not over the rooms of the lower story. The upper stories, therefore, recede, so that the building presents a terraced or pyramidal profile. One building at Tikal is five stories in height, in three receding planes, the three uppermost stories being one above the other. In a tower at Palenque we have an example of four stories but this is unusual.

On top of the building proper, especially if it is a temple, we frequently find a superstructure. This is a sort of crest, or roof wall, usually pierced by windows. When this wall rises from the center line of the roof it is called a roof comb or roof crest, and when it rises from the front wall it is called a flying façade. The highest temples in the Mayan Area are those of Tikal that attain a total height of about 175 feet, counting pyramid and superstructure.

Massive Sculptural Art. The decoration of Mayan buildings may be considered under three heads: first, interior decoration; second, façade decoration; third, supplementary monuments. In many temples at Yaxchilan, Tikal, etc., are found splendidly sculptured lintels of stone or wood. At Copan we see wall sculptures that adorn the entrance to the sanctuary and at Palenque finely sculptured tablets let into the rear wall of the sanctuary. Elsewhere are occasional examples of mural paintings, sculptured door jambs, decorated interior steps, etc.

The façade decorations of the earlier Mayan structures are freer and more realistic than those of the later buildings. In many cases they consist of figures of men, serpents, etc., modeled in stucco

or built up out of several nicely fitted blocks of
stone. Grotesque faces also occur. In the later
styles, decoration consists largely of "mask panels,"
which are grotesque front view faces arranged to
fill rectangular panels, but there is an increasing
amount of purely geometric ornament. The masked
panels represent in most instances a highly elaborated serpent's face which sometimes carries the

Fig. 22. Mask Panel over Doorway at Xkichmook. Yucatan.

special markings of one of the greater gods. These
panels, considered historically, pass through some
interesting developments. Angular representations
of serpent heads in profile are sometimes used at the
sides of doorways.

The supplementary monuments are stelæ and
altars. These are monolithic sculptures that are
often set up in definite relation to a building either
on the terraces or at the foot of the stairway. The
stelæ are great plinths or slabs of stone carved on
one or more sides with the figures of priests and
warriors loaded down with religious symbols. The
altars are small stones usually placed in front of the
stelæ. Many stelæ and altars are set up in plazas
and have no definite architectural quality.

[a]

[b]

Plate XVIII. (a) Realistic Designs on Vases from Chamá, Guatemala, representing the Best Mayan Period in Pottery; (b) The Quetzal as represented on a Painted Cylindrical Vase from Copan. Bands of hieroglyphs are commonly found on Mayan Pottery.

85

Fig. 23.   Design on Engraved Pot representing a Jaguar seated in a Wreath of Water Lilies.   Northern Yucatan.

Fig. 24.   Painted Design on Cylindrical Bowl showing Serpent issuing from a Shell.   Salvador.

Minor Arts. While the richly ornamented temples and the great monoliths attract first attention as works of art, the humbler products of the potter, the weaver, and the lapidary also attained to grace and dignity.

The Mayas were expert potters and employed a variety of technical processes in the decoration of their wares, such as painting, modeling, engraving, and stamping. We can only take time to examine a few examples of the best works, leaving the commoner products practically undescribed. Suffice it to say, that tripod dishes were much used, as well as bowls, bottle-necked vessels, and cylindrical vases, and that the common decorative use of hieroglyphs serves to mark off Mayan pottery from that of other Central American peoples. The realistic designs are drawn in accordance with the highest principles of decorative art. Serpents, monkeys, jaguars, various birds, as well as priests and supernatural beings, are used as subjects for pottery embellishment. Geometric decoration is also much used.

The polychrome pottery is rare and exceptionally beautiful, with designs relating to religious subjects. The background color of these cylindrical vases is usually orange or yellow, the designs are outlined in black, and the details filled in with delicate washes of red, brown, white, etc. The surface bears a high polish made by rubbing. Plate XVIII reproduces the design units on two vases from Chamá, Guatemala. The first example pictures a seated man with a widespreading headdress made of two conventional serpent heads from the ends of which issue the plumes of the quetzal. The hieroglyphs are Mayan day signs—Ben and Imix on the

left and Kan and Caban on the right. The second
example presents a god before an altar. This god
has the face of an old man and his body is attached
to a spiral shell. This divinity was probably associated with the end of the year.

In the next illustration an engraved design on a
bowl from northern Yucatan is given. A jaguar

Fig. 25. Mayan Basket represented in Stone Sculpture.

attired in the dress of man is seated in a wreath
of water lilies. After the vessel had been formed,
but before it had been fired, this design was made
by cutting away the background and incising finer
details on the original surfaces. Other designs in
relief were obtained by direct modeling or by
stamping. The stamps were moulds or negatives
made from bas-relief patterns.

The textile arts of the ancient Mayas can be recovered in part from a study of the monuments since
the designs on many garments are reproduced in
delicate relief. The designs are mostly all-over
geometric patterns, but borders reproducing the
typical "celestial band," a line of astronomical
symbols, are also seen. The techniques of brocade
and lace were understood by the ancient weavers.
In the minor textile art of basketry the products
must also have ranked high; a typical basket pictured on a lintel is given in Fig. 25.

Jade and other semi-precious stones were carved by the Mayas into beautiful and fantastic shapes. There was a considerable use of mosaic veneer on masks and other ceremonial objects. Metal was unknown during the first centuries of Mayan florescence, later it was rare and could not be used for tools, but the working of gold and copper in the manufacture of ornaments was on a high plane.

Having now passed in brief review the objective side of Mayan remains, let us turn our attention to the subjective.

The Serpent in Mayan Art. Mayan art is strange and unintelligible at first sight, but after careful study many wonderful qualities appear in it. In the knowledge of foreshortening and composition, the Mayas were superior to the Egyptians and Assyrians. They could draw the human body in pure profile and in free and graceful attitudes and they could compose several figures in a rectangular panel so that the result satisfies the eye of a modern artist.

But, unfortunately for our fuller understanding, the human form had only a minor interest because the gods were not in the image of man and the art was essentially religious. The gods were at best half human and half animal with grotesque elaborations. The high esthetic qualities were therefore wasted on subjects that appear trivial to many of us. But, as we break away more and more from the shackles of our own artistic conventions, we shall be able to appreciate the many beauties of ancient American sculpture.

The serpent motive controlled the character of Mayan art and was of first importance in all subsequent arts in Central America and Mexico. The serpent was seldom represented realistically, and yet we may safely infer that the rattlesnake was the prevailing model. Parts of other creatures were added to the serpent's body, such as the plumes of the trogon or quetzal, the teeth of the jaguar, and the ornaments of man. The serpent was idealized

Fig. 26. Typical Elaborated Serpents of the Mayas. The serpent with a human head in its mouth is from Yaxchilan. In this example the writhing movements of the serpent's tail are probably intended by the added scrolls. The plumed serpent is from Chichen Itza.

and the lines characteristic of it entered into the delineation of many subjects distinct from the serpent itself. Scrolls and other sinuous details were attached to the serpent's body and human ornaments such as earplugs, noseplugs, and even headdresses were added to its head. Finally, a human head was placed in the distended jaws. The Mayas may have intended to express the essential human

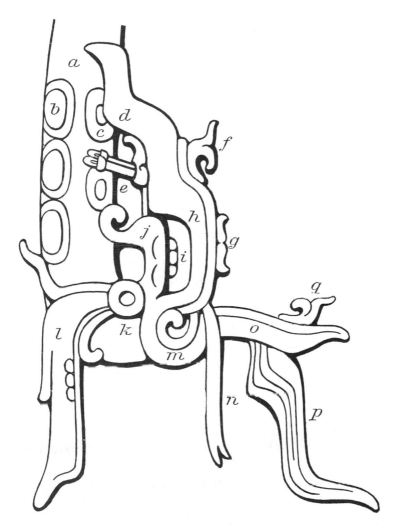

Fig. 27. Conventional Serpent of the Mayas used for Decorative Purposes: *a*, body; *b*, ventral scale; *c*, dorsal scale; *d*, nose; *e*, nose-plug; *f*, incisor tooth; *g*, molar tooth; *h*, jaw; *i*, eye; *j*, supraorbital plate; *k*, earplug; *l*, ear pendant; *m*, curled fang; *n*, tongue, *o*, lower jaw; *p*, beard; *q*, incisor tooth.

intelligence of the serpent in this fashion. The
serpent with a human head in its mouth doubtless
belongs in the same category as the partly humanized gods of Egypt, Assyria, and India. It illustrates the partial assumption of human form by a
beast divinity. The features combined are so pecu-

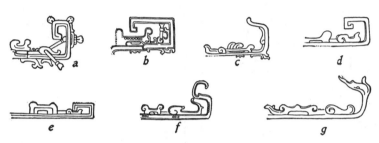

Fig. 28.   Upper Part of Serpent Head made into a Fret Orna-
ment; *a*, Ixkun; *b*, Quirigua; *c*, *d*, *g*, Copan; *e*, Naranjo; *f*, Seibal.

liar and unnatural that the influence of Mayan art
can be traced far and wide through Central America
and Mexico by comparative study of the serpent
motive.

A typical serpent head in profile (with the human
head omitted) as developed by the Mayas for decorative purposes is reproduced in Fig. 27 with the
parts lettered and named. It will be noted that the
lines of interest in this design are either vertical or
horizontal, although the parts themselves have sinuous outlines. Two features of the typical serpent's
body enter widely into the enrichment of all kinds of
subjects. One of these is the double outline which
is derived from the line paralleling the base of the
serpent's body and serving to mark off the belly
region. The second feature is the small circle applied in bead-like rows to represent scales. The
profile serpent head is also seen in scrolls and frets

that elaborate many details of dress worn by the human beings carved on the monuments. The front view of the serpent's head is usually extended to fill an oblong panel and is often used to decorate the base of a monument or the façade of a building. There are several monsters closely connected with the serpent that will be discussed as the description proceeds.

The Human Figure. The human beings pictured on Mayan monuments are captives, rulers, and priests or worshippers. The captives are poor groveling creatures, bound by rope, held by the hair or crushed under foot to fill a rectangular space over

Fig. 29. Sculpture on Front of Lintel at Yaxchilan showing Man holding Two-Headed Serpent with a Grotesque God's Head in each of its Mouths.

which the conqueror stands. The rulers and priests are hard to distinguish from each other, perhaps because the government was largely theocratic and the ruler was looked upon as the spokesman of divinity. The spear and shield of war served to mark off certain human beings from others who carry religious objects such as the Ceremonial Bar and the Manikin Scepter.

Elaborate thrones on several monuments are canopied over by the arched body of the Two-headed Dragon that bears symbols of the planets. Over all is seen the great Serpent Bird with outstretched wings. Upon the throne is seated a human being who may safely be called a king and a line of footprints on the front of the throne may symbolize ascent. On other monuments the commanding personage wears the mask of a god and wields a club to

Fig. 30.   Types of Human Heads on the Lintels of Yaxchilan.

subdue or scatters grain to placate. On the great majority of monuments the human beings, richly attired in ceremonial regalia and carrying a variety of objects, possibly present the great warriors and priests of the day. Many of the early sculptures are stiff and formal, but in a number of instances the quality of actual portraiture is convincing.

Design, Composition, and Perspective. It is difficult to compare directly the graphic and plastic arts of different nations where the subject matter is diverse unless we compare them in accordance with absolute principles of design, composition, and perspective drawing. The Mayas produced one of the few really great and coherent expressions of beauty so far given to the world and their influence in America was historically as important as was that of the Greeks in Europe. Set as we are in the matrix of our own religious and artistic conventions,

we find it difficult to approach sympathetically
beauty that is overcast with an incomprehensible religion. When we can bring ourselves to feel the
serpent symbolism of the Mayan artists as we feel,

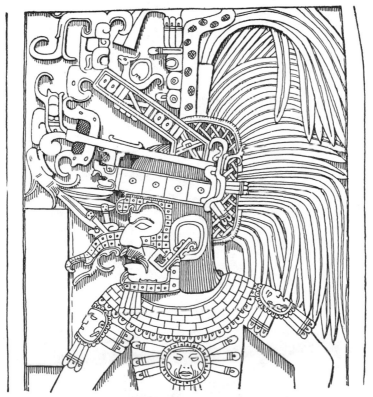

Fig. 31. Sculpture on Upper Part of Stela 11, Seibal. The man
wears an inlaid mask, an elaborate headdress, and a collar of shell
and jade.

for instance, the conventional halo that crowns the
ideal head of Christ, then we shall be able to recog-
nize the truly emotional qualities of Mayan sculptures.

Plate XIX. Stela 13, Piedras Negras. This shattered monument is one of the finest examples of Mayan sculpture, showing a fine sense of composition and a considerable knowledge of perspective. Dated March 27, 511 A. D.

It is generally recognized that design to be successful must contain order of various sorts (in measurements, shapes, directions, tones, colors, etc.). In the simpler forms of decorative art the restrictions of technical process, as in basketry, may impose order, but in freehand sculpture it must come from an educated sense of beauty involving selection and the reproduction of the finest qualities. Design at its highest is embodied in the Mayan hieroglyphs. Given spaces had to be filled with given symbols and the results attained were uniformly excellent. Although the influence of the serpent led to the great use of tapering flame-like masses in nearly all Mayan designs, still dominant vertical and horizontal lines of interest were maintained.

The panel and lintel sculptures show composition achieved by simple and subtle methods. The sweeping plumes of headdresses were skilfully used to fill in corners, while blocks of glyphs were placed in open spaces that might otherwise distract the attention. Many compositions appear overcrowded to us, but this fault decreases with knowledge of the subject matter. Also, the Mayas appear to have painted their sculptures so that the details were emphasized by color contrast.

In perspective as applied to the human figure the Mayas were far ahead of the Egyptians and Assyrians, since they could draw the body in front view and pure profile without the distortions seen in the Old World. They were even able to make graceful approximations of a three-quarters view, as may be seen in Plate XIX, where the raising of the nearer shoulder has a distinct perspective value.

The Mayan Pantheon. We have seen that during the earliest culture of Mexico and Central America there were no figurines of individualized gods, simply straightforward representations of human beings and animals. With the Mayan culture, however, we enter upon an epoch of rich religious symbolism. The serpent, highly conventionalized as we have just seen, and variously combined with elements taken from the quetzal, the jaguar, and even

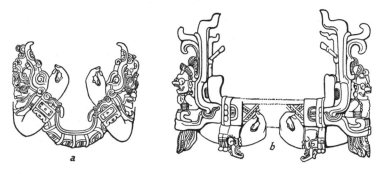

Fig. 32. The Ceremonial Bar. A Two-Headed Serpent held in the Arms of Human Beings on Stelæ: *a*, Stela P, Copan; *b*, Stela N, Copan.

from man himself, appears as a general indication of divinity. The Ceremonial Bar, essentially a two-headed serpent carrying in its mouths the heads of an important god, is one of the earliest religious objects. The heads that appear in the mouths are usually those of a Roman-nosed or of a Long-nosed god. Other representations of divinities are combined with the Two-headed Dragon that also has reptilian characters; still others appear as head-dresses and masks on human figures. Strange to say, the gods are supplementary to the human figures on all the early sculptures. In the codices, however, they are represented apart from man, as engaged in various activities and contests. Mayan religion was clearly organized on a dualistic basis. The powers for good are in a constant struggle with the powers for evil and most of the benevolent divinities have malevolent duplicates. In actual form the gods are partly human, but ordinarily the determining features are grotesque variations from the human face and figure. While beast associations are sometimes discernible, they are rarely controlling. Sometimes, however, beast gods are represented in unmistakable fashion, good examples being the jaguar, the bat, and the moan bird. All of these have human bodies and animal heads.

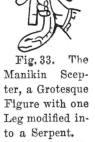

Fig. 33. The Manikin Scepter, a Grotesque Figure with one Leg modified into a Serpent.

The head position in the Mayan pantheon may with some assurance be given to a god who has been called the Roman-nosed god and who is probably to be identified with Itzamna. According to Spanish writers Itzamna was regarded by the Mayas as the creator and father of all, the inventor of writing, the founder of the Mayan civilization, and the god of light and life. This Zeus of the Mayas is represented in the form of an old man with a high forehead, a strongly aquiline nose, and a distended mouth, toothless, or with a single enlarged tooth in front. On the ancient monuments he is frequently seen in the mouths of the Ceremonial Bar and also in association with the sun, moon, and the planet Venus. In the codices he is shown as a protector of the Maize God and in other acts beneficial to

man. There is, however, a malevolent aspect of
this god or possibly another being who imitates his
features but not his qualities. This being may be
an old woman goddess who wears a serpent headdress and who is associated with destructive floods,
the very opposite of life-giving sunshine.

Of almost equal importance to the Roman-nosed
god is a god whose face is a more or less humanized
serpent. His proper name is Ah Bolon Dzacab.

Fig. 34. The Two-Headed Dragon, a Monster that passes
through many Forms in Mayan Sculpture. It apparently sym-
bolizes calamities at inferior conjunction of Venus and the Sun.
Copan.

On the early monuments this god is shown in connection with the Ceremonial Bar. He also appears
at a somewhat later date as the Manikin Scepter,
an object in the form of a manikin that is held out
by a leg modified into a serpent's body. Since a
celt is usually worn in the forehead of the manikin
it has been suggested that this curious object represents a ceremonial battle-ax. The face of the Long-
nosed god is frequently worn by high priests and
rulers either as a headdress or, more rarely, as a
mask. It is possible that this divinity was regarded
as primarily a war god but in the codices he is
evidently a universal deity of varied powers. Especially he is shown in connection with water and
maize and it seems likely that his principal function

was to cause life-giving rain. A malevolent variant of the Long-nosed god has a bare bone for the lower jaw, a sun symbol on his forehead, and a headdress consisting of three other symbols. This head is associated with the Two-headed Dragon, a monster which brings calamity at times of the inferior conjunction of Venus and the Sun.

Ah Puch, the Lord of Death, was the principal malevolent god. His body as figured in the codices is a strange compound of skeletal and full-fleshed parts. His head is a skull except for the normal

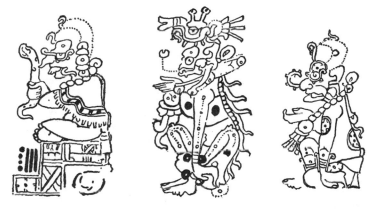

Fig. 35. Gods in the Dresden Codex: God B, the Long-Nosed God of Rain; God A, the Death God; God G, the Sun God.

ears. His spinal column is usually bare and sometimes the ribs as well, but the arms and legs are often covered with flesh. As added symbols black spots and dotted lines are sometimes drawn upon his body and a curious device like a percentage sign upon his cheek. The Death God in complete form is rarely shown in the earlier sculptures, although grinning skulls and interlacing bones occur as tem-

[a]

[b]

Plate XX. (a) Top of Stela 1 at Yaxchilan, dealing with the Heavens. The Sky God is seen in the center with the moon at the left and the sun at the right. Below these is the Two-Headed Dragon bearing planet signs and additional heads of the Sky God; (b) Analogous Detail of Stela 4, Yaxchilan. The moon is at the right and the sun at the left. The figure in the sun is male and that in the moon, female. The faces of the Sky God hang from the lower part of the Two-Headed Dragon, being attached to it by symbols of the planet Venus.

102

ple decorations. As has already been pointed out, Mayan religion was strongly dualistic and the evil powers are usually to be identified by death symbols such as a bare bone for the lower jaw, or the percentage symbol noted above on the cheek. Death heads of several kinds are frequent in the hieroglyphic inscriptions.

The Maize God, figured so frequently on the ancient monuments and in the Mayan codices may be the same that in the time of the Conquest was called Yum Kaax, Lord of the Harvest. He is represented as a youth with a leafy headdress that is possibly meant to represent an opening ear of maize. The *kan* sign, a grain of maize, is constantly associated with him. He appears to be at the mercy of the evil deities when not protected by the good ones.

Space considerations forbid a further study of Mayan gods. Suffice it to say that several other divinities are shown in the sculptures and codices including a somewhat youthful appearing war god, as well as a more mature and grotesque war god called Ek Ahau, the Black Captain. There is an old god with a shell attached to his body, a god with the face of a monkey who is associated with the North Star, a god in the form of a frog and another in the form of a bat. In the Spanish accounts we can also glean scanty information concerning Ixchel, Goddess of the Rainbow and mate of Itzamna; Ixtubtun, patroness of jade carvers; Ixchebelyax, patroness of the art of weaving and decorating cloth, etc.

How Mayan History has been Recovered. The arrangement of Mayan remains on a time scale is now an accomplished fact thanks to a correlation which permits us to read the dates on ancient monuments in terms of the Gregorian calendar and the Christian era. Early attempts to achieve this result met with widely varying results. Most of these attempts were made by developing a single line of evidence and some were based on assumptions that can now be disproved. But no single line of evidence should be deemed sufficient to decide this all important question.

The general course of Mayan history is indicated unmistakably by four principal lines of evidence capable of being correlated with each other. These are:—

1. Stratigraphic sequences in pottery, stylistic sequences in sculpture, structural sequences in architecture, etc.

2. Traditional history preserved in the Books of Chilam Balam and representing a knowledge of past events at the time of the Spanish Conquest.

3. Dates inscribed on a great number of monuments in terms of the ancient Mayan time counts.

4. Astronomical checks on these inscribed dates.

The artistic position of a monument may be used to validate the contemporaneous character of an inscribed date, otherwise interpretable as referring to the past or future, or it may serve to fix a repeating date in a single historical setting. The events in the traditional history of the Books of Chilam Balam, meager enough when taken alone, have the valuable quality of reaching back into the time of the First Empire when the use of dates on temples and monuments was much in vogue. They permit a richly documented past to be tied in, as it were, to a poorly documented terminal period.

Before the matter of the ancient inscribed dates

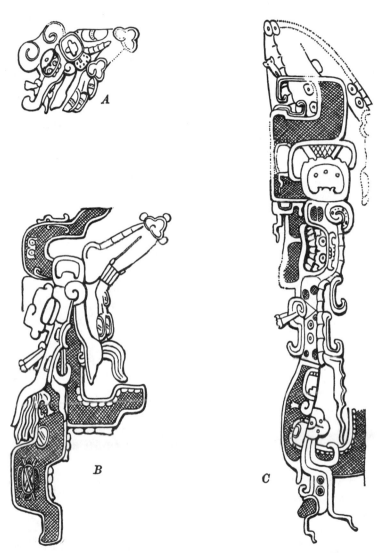

Fig. 36. The Front Head of the Two-Headed Dragon on Stelæ at Piedras Negras showing the Increase in Flamboyant Treatment. The interval between (a) and (b) is 125 years, that between (b) and (c) is 45 years.

can be understood, however, the somewhat complicated mechanism of the Mayan calendar must be
explained, as well as the system of hieroglyphs and
the notation of numbers.   Then there is the problem
of correlation which necessitates delicate adjudica-
tions of evidence.   Finally we must take up the
proofs which demonstrate the astronomical achievements of the Mayas which, in reverse, provide
checks upon the correctness of the day for day
correlation itself.   We must proceed slowly and
carefully, without much following of by-ways, however attractive they may appear.   We will begin
with stratigraphy and stylistic sequence.

Sequences in Art.   The study of Mayan ceramics
reveals developments as regard shapes, fabrics, and
designs.   Specimens recovered from sealed cysts
under stelæ at Copan establish true associations
with the higher forms of art and can be used far
and wide in comparison with pottery finds in Salvador, Guatemala, etc.   Vaillant has found stratigraphic sequences in a collection of funerary vessels
obtained at Holmul, where graves occurred under
the floors and within the filled-in chambers of a
buried temple.

As regards sculpture we find at Copan a remarkably homogeneous series of stelæ on which a royal
or priestly personage stands erect and in front view.
A Ceremonial Bar is held symmetrically in the two
arms and the body is partly covered with rich and
elaborate ornament.   The amount of relief, the proportions of the body, the forms of the Ceremonial
Bar, etc., all pass through a harmonious development.   The earliest monuments show a crude block-
like carving of the face, with protruding eyes, while
the latest monuments have fully rounded contours.

Plate XXI. Development in Style of Carving at Copan. Left to right: Stela 9 (9.10.10.0.0, 383 A. D.); Stela 5 (9.13.15.0.0, 447 A. D.); Stela N (9.16.10.0.0, 502 A. D.); Stela H (9.17.12.0.0, 523 A. D.); Bottom: Details of architecture showing analogous development.

At Tikal the stelæ show, for the most part, human figures in profile, but unmistakable development can be seen in general quality of carving as well as in specific details.

In making comparisons in art it is always necessary to consider similar things. At many other Mayan cities than the two named above it is possible to obtain satisfactory evidence of sequence in art forms by cutting out similar details from different masses. Thus at Naranjo, when we examine all the Ceremonial Bars, we find a remarkable development of flamboyant detail on the later monuments. At Quirigua the faces on the tops of the altars may be compared with the same result. At Piedras Negras the heads of the Two-headed Dragon that occur in exactly similar positions on four monuments likewise show a steady modification towards flamboyancy as may be seen from Fig. 36, where the front heads are put side by side.

Fig. 37. Grotesque Face on the Back of Stela B, Copan.

Fig. 38. Jaguar in Dresden Codex with a Water Lily attached to Forehead.

Still other lines of evidence on historical sequence are to be gained from a study of architecture. Not only is it possible to determine the general developments that hold true of the entire Mayan Area but also in a given city it is sometimes possible to arrange the buildings in their order of erection according to dependable criteria, both decorative and structural.

The earliest temples have narrow vaulted r o o m s, heavy walls, and a single doorway. The rooms increase in width, the walls decrease in thickness, the doorways multiply till the spaces between them become piers and finally columns. The support for the heavy roof comb taxed the structural ingenuity of the Mayan architects. T h e solving of this problem is marked by successive advances and since mechanical science goes forward rather than backward the

Fig. 39. Late Sculpture from Chichen Itza. The head-dress resembles that worn by the rulers on the highlands of Mexico.

relative order of structures is fairly certain. Moreover, many buildings are closely associated with dated monuments, tablets, lintels, or stelæ. Still another evidence of architectural sequence is seen in structures that have been enlarged by the addition of wings or by the enclosing of the old parts under new masonry.

Books of Chilam Balam. We now turn to a very different kind of history, the digests of ancient chronicles in the Mayan language but in Spanish

script which managed to survive in the so-called
Books of Chilam Balam along with other texts, ceremonial and medical.   There are five chronicles, the
two longest covering 68 katuns before the coming of
the Spaniards in 1517.   We now know that these
katuns were time units consisting of 7200 days, or
nearly 20 years, and that they were designated by
their final day which was always a day called Ahau
associated with a number, 1 and 13, in a peculiar
sequence.   A katun with the same designation returns in 13 × 7200 days or about 256 years.   Such
a completion, counted especially from a Katun 8
Ahau, was called the "doubling back of the katuns"
or, as we would say, the completion of a cycle.   The
count of the katuns used in the chronicles was really
part and parcel of a fuller count just as a year '22
implies a position in one of the centuries of our
Christian era.

The chronicles unfortunately give few names of
chieftains and cities and few outstanding events.
Chichen Itza is the city most fully concerned and
an early occupation is recorded, then an abandonment for some two and a half centuries.   After its
re-establishment the Toltecs enter Yucatan and
capture this capital.   The first part of the chronicles has the atmosphere of myth rather than history,
but a calendarial adjustment of some kind is mentioned in one place.   This was an event which took
place in 503 A. D. as we shall see in another place.

The first rough correlation between the time count
on the ancient monuments and the time count in the
chronicles was made on the theory that a dated
lintel at Chichen Itza had to be placed in the first
occupation of the city: when this was done the beginning of the chronicles was found to proceed from

an important round number in the old day count while the abandonment of Chichen Itza coincided with the abandonment of all the cities of the Mayan First Empire.   We must now turn attention to the famous calendar.

The Mayan Time Counts.   The passage of time, seen in finer and finer degree in the course of human life, the succession of summer and winter, the waxing and waning moons, the alternation of day and night, the upward and downward sloping of the sun, and the swinging dial of the stars, are phenomena that no human group has failed to notice.   Longer periods than those included within the memory of the oldest men (presenting an imperfect reflection of the memory of men still older) are found only in those favored centers where a serviceable system of counting has been developed.   Mythology has a content of history but hardly of chronology.   Tradition, when organized by the priesthood, may be reasonably dependable for perhaps two hundred years.

The year and the month are the basis of all primitive time systems, the former depending on the recurring seasons, the latter on recurring moons. Both of these are expressed in days.   Unfortunately, the day is not contained evenly in either the month or the year, nor do these larger time measures show any simple relation to each other as regards length. The history of the calendar is one of compromise and correction.

The Mayan calendars were made possible by: first, the knowledge of astronomical time periods; second, the possession of a suitable notation system; third, the discovery of a permutation system of names and numbers.

Elements of the Day Count. There is reason to believe that the Mayas had first a lunar-solar calendar of twelve months of thirty days each, making a year of 360 days, and that they reduced the number of days in the formal month to 20 and raised the number of months in the year from 12 to 18. These changes permitted a close adjustment of the units of time with their vigesimal system of counting. With a truer knowledge of the length of the

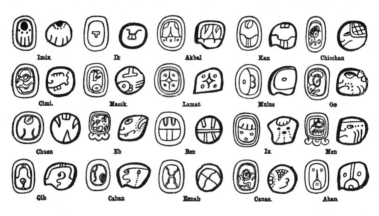

Fig. 40. The Twenty Day Signs. The first example in each case is taken from the inscriptions and the second from the codices.

year an extra five day month was added to make a year of 365 days. Beyond this the "leap year" error was calculated but not interpolated. As proof that the lunar month of thirty days preceded the formal month of twenty days, it need only be pointed out that the name for this period, *uinal*, seems to be connected with the name for moon, *u*, and that the hieroglyph for moon has the value, twenty, in the inscriptions and ancient books.

Before entering into a fuller discussion of the astronomical and notational facts let us turn for a moment to the third fact, the permutation system. The origin of the cycle [1] known by the Mayan name *tzolkin* and the Aztecan name *tonalamatl*, book of the days, has never been satisfactorily explained. It is a permutation system with two factors, 13 and 20. The former is a series of numbers (1–13) and the latter a series of twenty names as follows:—

1. Imix	6. Cimi	11. Chuen	16. Cib
2. Ik	7. Manik	12. Eb	17. Caban
3. Akbal	8. Lamat	13. Ben	18. Eznab
4. Kan	9. Muluc	14. Ix	19. Cauac
5. Chicchan	10. Oc	15. Men	20. Ahau

These two series revolve upon each other like two wheels, one with thirteen and the other with twenty cogs. The smaller wheel of numbers makes twenty revolutions while the larger wheel of days is making thirteen revolutions, and after this the number cog and name cog with which the experiment began are again in combination. Thus, a day with the same number and the same name recurs every 13×20 or 260 days.

This 260 day cycle corresponds to no natural time period and is an invention pure and simple. It is the most fundamental feature of the Mayan time count and of the time counts of other nations in Mexico and Central America. We may perhaps assume that the twenty names were originally those of the twenty days in the modified lunar months. But the thirteen numbers have no recognized prototype. The formal book of days generally was con-

[1] The word *cycle* is applied in this book to re-entering series, or wheels, of days. These all contain the *tzolkin* or *tonalamatl* without a remainder. The word *period* is applied to fixed numbers that do not contain the *tonalamatl*.

sidered to begin with 1 Imix for the Mayas and with a corresponding day for the other Mexican and Central American nations. But it can be made to begin anywhere and proceed to an equivalent station that is always 260 days removed.

PERMUTATION TABLE

		1	2	3	4	5	6	7	8	9	10	11	12	13	1
1	Imix	1	8	2	9	3	10	4	11	5	12	6	13	7	1
2	Ik	2	9	3	10	4	11	5	12	6	13	7	1	8	2
3	Akbal	3	10	4	11	5	12	6	13	7	1	8	2	9	3
4	Kan	4	11	5	12	6	13	7	1	8	2	9	3	10	4
5	Chicchan	5	12	6	13	7	1	8	2	9	3	10	4	11	5
6	Cimi	6	13	7	1	8	2	9	3	10	4	11	5	12	6
7	Manik	7	1	8	2	9	3	10	4	11	5	12	6	13	7
8	Lamat	8	2	9	3	10	4	11	5	12	6	13	7	1	8
9	Muluc	9	3	10	4	11	5	12	6	13	7	1	8	2	9
10	Oc	10	4	11	5	12	6	13	7	1	8	2	9	3	10
11	Chuen	11	5	12	6	13	7	1	8	2	9	3	10	4	11
12	Eb	12	6	13	7	1	8	2	9	3	10	4	11	5	12
13	Ben	13	7	1	8	2	9	3	10	4	11	5	12	6	13
14	Ix	1	8	2	9	3	10	4	11	5	12	6	13	7	1
15	Men	2	9	3	10	4	11	5	12	6	13	7	1	8	2
16	Cib	3	10	4	11	5	12	6	13	7	1	8	2	9	3
17	Caban	4	11	5	12	6	13	7	1	8	2	9	3	10	4
18	Eznab	5	12	6	13	7	1	8	2	9	3	10	4	11	5
19	Cauac	6	13	7	1	8	2	9	3	10	4	11	5	12	6
20	Ahau	7	1	8	2	9	3	10	4	11	5	12	6	13	7

The Conventional Year. It has been stated that the Mayas arrived at a conventional 365 day year made up of eighteen months of twenty days each plus a short period of five days that fell after the eighteen regular months had been counted. The Mayan month names are as follows:—

1. Pop	7. Yaxkin	13. Mac
2. Uo	8. Mol	14. Kankin
3. Zip	9. Chen	15. Muan
4. Zotz	10. Yax	16. Pax
5. Tzec	11. Zac	17. Kayab
6. Xul	12. Ceh	18. Cumhu

19. Uayeb (five additional days)

Since there are twenty days or positions in the month and likewise twenty distinct day names in the *tzolkin,* falling in regular order, it follows that each day would always occupy the same month position

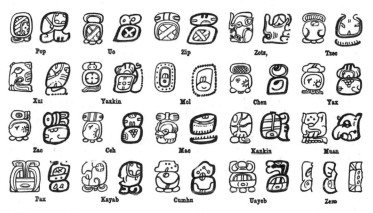

Fig. 41. The Nineteen Month Signs of the Mayan Year. The first example in each case is taken from the inscriptions and the second from the codices. The last details are signs for zero.

were it not for the offset at the end of each year caused by the short Uayeb period. As it is, any day name occupies the same month position during the course of an entire year and a position five days in advance during the course of the following year. Since five is contained four times in twenty there can be only four shifts, the fifth year showing the same arrangement as the first. The following table

Plate XXII. Scheme of the Mayan Calendar as presented in the Codex Tro-Cortesianus. In the center is Itzamna, the God of the Sky, and his spouse, under what has been called the celestial tree. The band of hieroglyphs that frames in this picture contains the twenty day signs of the Mayan month. The figures on the outside are arranged in four groups, according to the four directions of the compass. At the top or east we again see Itzamna and his mate. In the north, or right hand quarter, human sacrifice is shown and the Death God sits opposite the God of War. In the east and in the south are also shown pairs of divinities. A series of dots running from one day sign to another covers the *tzolkin* or 260 day cycle of names and numbers.

116

gives the month positions of each day name during the changes of four consecutive years as these are recorded in the ancient inscriptions.

Ik	Manik	Eb	Caban	0	5	10	15
Akbal	Lamat	Ben	Eznab	1	6	11	16
Kan	Muluc	Ix	Cauac	2	7	12	17
Chicchan	Oc	Men	Ahau	3	8	13	18
Imix	Cimi	Chuen	Cib	4	9	14	19

Thus Ik occupies 0 position the first year, 5, the second year, 10 the third, 15 the fourth, and 0 the fifth. While Manik that belongs to the same set has position 5 the first year, 10 the second, etc. It will be noted that Imix, the first day of the formal permutation of the *tzolkin* is never the first day of a month.

The Calendar Round. But this assignment of particular day names to particular places in the month does not close the problem. Each day name is associated in the *tzolkin,* or permutation, with a day number. While it is true that each day can occupy only four month positions in as many years, it must be remembered that the day numbers associated with these names can run the whole gamut of 13 changes. Thus, although Ik must always occupy the fifth position in the months during a certain year, nevertheless it will have numbers which fall in the sequence 1, 8, 2, 9, 3, 10, 4, 11, 5, 12, 6, 13, 1, etc. The complete cycle of variations must run through the least common multiple of 260 (the permutation) and 365 (the conventional year) or 18,980 days. This cycle is commonly known as the Calendar Round. A Mayan day fixed in a month, or let us say a calendar round date, has four parts to its name, thus, 11 Ahau 18 Mac. We describe a day as Tuesday, July 4, meaning "Tuesday the third day of the seven day week occupies the fourth position in the month of July." Similarly the Mayan date 11 Ahau 18 Mac may be read "the day named Ahau as eleventh day in a thirteen day week occupies the eighteenth position in the month Mac." Owing to leap year corrections the European date given above does not recur at regular intervals, but a Mayan day recurs infallibly in 52 calendar years, never sooner, never later.

So far we have considered two kinds of Mayan dates, first the *tzolkin* date, recurring every 260 days, secondly the calendar round date recurring every 18,980 days. Before we can understand a third and much more important kind of date, namely a date which states, in addition to the calendar round designation, the total number of days since a beginning day called 4 Ahau 8 Cumhu, located far in the past, we must direct our attention to the matter of numbers and notation.

Mayan Numbers. The three most common numerical systems in use in the world are all derived from man's anatomy. The quinary system is based on counting the fingers of one hand, the decimal system on counting those of both hands and the vigesimal system, which prevailed in Central America, is based on counting all the fingers and all the toes. The vigesimal system is seen in imperfect form in our count of scores, where seventy years are three score and ten.

The Mayan name for one was *hun:* they had simple names to 9 and composite ones from 10 to 19, much as in English, and twenty was *hun kal,* one score. The ascending values in the vigesimal scale were as follows:—

Mayan Numbers			Arabic Equivalents
	hun		1
20 hun	=1	kal	20
20 kal	=1	bak	400
20 bak	=1	pic	8,000
20 pic	=1	cabal	160,000
20 cabal	=1	kinchil	3,200,000
20 kinchil	=1	alau	64,000,000
20 alau	=1	hablat	1,280,000,000

They invented signs for zero and discovered the principle of "local value" in the writing down of numbers centuries before these ideas (which are

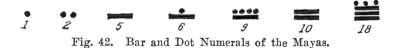

Fig. 42.   Bar and Dot Numerals of the Mayas.

fundamental to higher mathematics) were known in the Old World. The notation of numbers had its simpler and more complicated phase. In the simpler phase 1 was represented by a dot, 2 by two dots, 5 by a bar, 6 by a bar and dot, 15 by three bars, etc. The commonest sign for zero was a shell while a picture of the moon stood for twenty. In the more elaborate notation a series of twenty faces of gods represented the numerals from 0 to 19.

The straight vigesimal system was doubtless used by the Mayas in ordinary counting, but in counting time a very important change was introduced in the third position. Also the names were modified: *hun* was called *kin* which means sun or day. In the second position *kal* was called *uinal* which means month and 18 of these were taken to form a *tun,* stone, which was the third unit. The *tun* then had a value of 18 × 20 = 360 days, making a conventional year about five and a quarter days less than a true

year. Twenty *tuns* made a *kaltun* or *katun* and
above this period the numeral system proceeded as
before and in the ascending values the names already given were merely combined with *tun,* if
Gates is right in his clever suggestion. For years
it has been customary to speak of the fifth period
as cycle for want of a native term: this will
now be called *baktun.* One *hablatun,* the highest
period with a name, has the astonishing value of
460,800,000,000 days. However, the highest numbers fall considerably short of this potential limit.

In our decimal system the number 347,981, for
instance, is really:—

$$3 \times 100000$$
$$4 \times 10000$$
$$7 \times 1000$$
$$9 \times 100$$
$$8 \times 10$$
$$1 \times 1$$

When written out in a horizontal line each "position" has a value ten times that of the "position"
to the right of it. It is understood that a digit
which stands in a "position" is to be multiplied by
1, 10, 100, 1000, etc., as the case may be. The
Mayas, using the principle of position, ordinarily
write their bar and dot numerals in columns. But
we can partially transcribe a Mayan number in
imitation of our own system by putting dots or
dashes between the positions or periods. The number in five positions given below is transcribed as
9.12.16.7.8.

9 × 144000	1,296,000
12 × 7200	86,400
16 × 360	5,760
7 × 20	140
8 × 1	8
	1,388,308

We read this date: 9 baktuns, 12 katuns, 16 tuns, 7 uinals, and 8 kins. It is convenient to remember that a tun is a little less than a year, a katun a little

Fig. 43. Face Numerals found in Mayan Inscriptions. In most cases these are the faces of gods. Reading from left to right: the values are 1, 3, 4, 5, 6, 9, 10.

less than 20 years and a baktun a little less than 400 years. But the count is really of days, not years.

Fig. 44. The Normal Forms of the Period Glyphs. Reading from left to right: baktun, katun, tun, uinal, kin.

Although the numerical values are expressed by position alone in some cases, in other cases use is made of Period Glyphs to make assurance doubly

Fig. 45. Face Forms of Period Glyphs. From left to right: introducing glyph, baktun, katun, tun, uinal, kin.

sure. These Period Glyphs represent the basic value of the positions which are to be multiplied by the accompanying numerals. For examples, see Figs. 44 and 45.

Introducing Glyph

Initial Series
1. 9 baktuns (cycles).
2. 14 katuns
3. 13 tuns (written 12 by error)
4. 4 uinals
5. 17 kins
6. 12 Caban (day) ·

Supplementary Series
7. glyph F
8. (a) glyph D, (b) glyph C
9. (a) glyph X, (b) glyph B
10. (a) glyph A (30 day lunar month)
10. (b) 5 Kayab (month)

Explanatory Series
11, 12, 13 and 14a, possibly explain the dates

Secondary Series
14b, 3 kins, 13 uinals
15a, 6 tuns (to be added)

Period Ending Date
16. 4 Ahau 13 Yax (9.15.0.0.0)

Plate XXIII.   Typical Mayan Inscription.

The Long Count. Many early monuments of the Mayas have inscriptions with an enlarged Introducing Glyph containing a variable element indicating the title or principal subject matter of the inscription. Next follows the number of elapsed days from the epoch of a Mundane Era. This starting point is uniformly the day 4 Ahau 8 Cumhu and the complete Initial Series date not only states the number of elapsed days, but also the name and number of the day reached and its position in a Mayan month.

The Initial Series is normally followed by a Supplementary Series which concerns the lunar calendar, and often there are numbers of days to be added to or subtracted from the Initial Series date: these are called Secondary Series. Also Period Ending dates are used, these being merely abbreviated dates which correspond to indicated round numbers in the day count.

The Initial Series analyzed in Plate XXIII actually records the number 1,401,217. This number does not, however, reach the day 12 Caban declared immediately after it or the month position 5 Kayab recorded in glyph 10b. When 13 tuns are corrected to 12 tuns on the theory that the sculptor did not follow copy, we do reach 12 Caban 5 Kayab. Another check comes when we add the Secondary Series of 2423 days and reach 4 Ahau 13 Yax ending an even katun.

Dates of Dedication. Initial Series dates are especially common on stelæ at cities of the First Empire, mostly located in the southern part of the Mayan Area. While it is impossible to read much of the texts which accompany these dates nevertheless it is a remarkable fact that when we arrange the monuments in their artistic order we find that the inscribed dates in the great majority of cases fall in the same order. This leads us to conclude that the dates are practically contemporaneous with the carving and setting up of the monuments. Now the above is especially true when the inscription gives a simple Initial Series date. When more than one date is given the historic one appears in most instances to be the latest, but in a few instances it appears to be a specially emphasized intermediate date. In addition, then, to contemporaneous dates there are some that refer to the past and others that refer to the future.

Some writers have assumed that the stelæ and other inscribed monuments were primarily time markers set up at the end of hotun (or five year) periods. This seems an unnecessarily narrow view. We can demonstrate that some inscriptions deal with astronomical facts covering long stretches of time. It is also apparent that many of the sculptures represent conquests and it is extremely likely that portraits of actual rulers are to be seen in certain carvings. It would be too much to expect events to happen regularly at the end of time periods and as a matter of fact we find at different cities repeated dates that do not occupy such positions. These repeated dates would seem to recall events of special importance to the city in question.

The running co-ordination between the apparent order of the artistic styles and inscribed dates permits us to measure very accurately the rate of change in art which was rapid, indeed, at certain times. The style of carving, on the other hand, enables us to put into definite 52 year periods many of the calendar round dates—if these are to be regarded as contemporaneous. The result is that for the First Empire, as it has been called, there is an exceedingly accurate chronology. After the fall and abandonment of the great southern cities dates are rare and we have to fall back upon remnants of history preserved after the coming of the Spaniards.

Hieroglyphs. Mayan hieroglyphs resemble the Egyptian and Chinese hieroglyphs only in being "sacred writing" that is not based upon an alphabet. The styles and symbols are entirely different. No Rosetta Stone has yet been discovered to give us inscriptions in more than one system of writing in Central America. The great use of hieroglyphic inscriptions on monuments was characteristic of the earlier period of Mayan history and at a later time the writing was reduced to books. Bishop Landa obtained what he supposed was a Mayan alphabet, but what he really obtained was a list of signs representing among other sounds the particular sounds he had asked for.

The phonetic use of syllables rather than of simple sounds or letters is probably an important feature of Mayan writing. Many hieroglyphs are pictographic and consist of abbreviated pictures of the thing intended or of some object connected with it. Often a head stands for the entire body. The following list practically exhausts our knowledge of Mayan hieroglyphs:—

1. The signs for the twenty named days of the calendar.
2. The signs for the nineteen months of the Mayan year.

3. The face signs for numbers from zero to nineteen inclusive.

4. Period glyphs in two styles for place values in the numerical notation.

5. The symbols for the four directions and for the colors associated with them.

6. The hieroglyphs of several gods and ceremonies.

7. The symbols of Heaven and Earth, the Sun, Moon, Venus, Mars, Jupiter, and a few astronomical phenomena such as conjunctions.

8. Hieroglyphs for special times of the year such as solstices and equinoxes.

9. Signs meaning era, or base from which a numerical count is made, completion, etc.

Some of these have recently been solved, thanks to mathematical and astronomical calculations, others rest on the calendarial forms given by Landa. There are some phonetic elements in Mayan writing and some ideographic elements. It seems likely that the gist of the Mayan inscriptions which deal with history will be solved in somewhat the same fashion as those that deal with astronomy. The matter is, however, most perplexing. So far not a single place name or personal name has been definitely recognized and translated. In spite of the hundreds of glyphs recovered at the sites called Copan and Palenque, for instance, we do not know the real names of these cities or even their symbols. We may expect to find signs referring to tribute and common objects of trade and others referring to birth, death, establishment, conquest, destruction, and other fundamentals of individual and social existence. These signs, taken with directives, con-

nectives, and dates, would make possible the re-
covery of the main facts of history. There seems
no possibility of purely literary inscriptions.
While progress necessarily will be slow there is
no reason for despair and without doubt the greater

Fig. 46. Hieroglyphs of the Four Directions: East, North,
West, South.

portion of Mayan inscriptions will finally be deciphered.

As an example of the phonetic use of signs in the
building up of hieroglyphs let us take the common
sign *kin*, meaning "sun." This sign appears regularly in the glyphs for the world directions east and
west, the Mayan names being *likin* and *chikin*, and
also in the month sign *Yaxkin*, and sometimes in
that for *Kankin*. It also appears as the sign for
the lowest period in the time count having the value

Fig. 47. Hieroglyphs containing the Phonetic Element *kin*:
a–b, kin; c, li-kin; d, chi-kin; e–f, yax-kin; g, kan-kin.

of a single day and called *kin* (Fig. 47). Now this
kin sign also appears in many undeciphered hieroglyphs and in some of these it seems likely that it
has a phonetic value. Other signs with definite
values in several glyphs are *yax, tun, zac,* etc. This
general method of writing is seen in more decipher-

able form among the Aztecs. The glosses of the early priests that have proved so great a help in the case of the Aztecan writing are absent from the few Mayan documents.

Codices. Only three ancient Mayan books or codices are known to exist and these are more or less incomplete. They have all been reproduced in facsimile and are known by the following names: Dresden Codex, Peresianus Codex, Tro-Cortesianus Codex.

These illuminated manuscripts are written on both sides of long strips of amatl paper, folded like Japanese screens. The paper was given a smooth surface by a coating of fine lime and the drawings were made in black and in various colors. From the early accounts we know that books were also written on prepared deerskin and upon bark. Concerning their subject matter we are told that the Mayas had many books upon civil and religious history, and upon rites, magic, and medicine. The three books named above have been carefully studied. They treat principally of the calendar and of associated religious ceremonies.

A page of the Dresden Codex containing some interesting calculations is reproduced herewith. The numbers with the digits one above the other are transcribed in two diagrams. In the upper diagram the bar and dot numerals are simply put over into Arabic numerals and the Mayan system of periods or positions is retained. In the lower diagram these numbers are reduced entirely to the Arabic system. The columns are lettered at the top, the hieroglyphs are counted off in sixteen rows at the left and the separate groupings of numbers are shown in five sections at the right.

Among the hieroglyphs the Venus sign is especially prominent. At the base of column B is given a number in five periods that, counted from the normal beginning day 4 Ahau 8 Cumhu leads again to this day which is recorded at the bottom of column A. The long number in column C, similarly counted from 4 Ahau 8 Cumhu, leads to 1 Ahau 18 Kayab, recorded at the bottom of B. The day 1 Ahau 18 Uo is reached by another calculation which will be explained later. At the base of A is a number in three periods which amounts to 2200. Not only is this the difference between the long numbers in B and C (1,366,560 — 1,364,360 = 2200) but it is also the number of days by which 1 Ahau 18 Kayab precedes 4 Ahau 8 Cumhu. In other words we deal in this passage with the end of the seventy-second calendar round after the original 4 Ahau 8 Cumhu and with a new point of departure 2200 days earlier, which is some way involved with the calendar of Venus.

Let us now make a new beginning in the lower left hand corner of this page. In G5 we find the number 2920 which as we have already seen is exactly the number of days consumed in eight years of 365 days or five synodic revolutions of Venus of 584 days. We will now see how the Mayan scholars arrived at 13 × 2920 or 37,960, the calendar round of Venus. If we proceed towards the left in section 5 we find the second number, F5, is 5840 which equals 2 × 2920, the third is 8760 or 3 × 2920, and the fourth is 11,680 or 4 × 2920. The addition is continued in sections 4 and 3 till we reach 35,040 or 12 × 2920. To be sure the scribe made a slight error in one place, writing a 5 for an 8 but this is caught up by the day signs 9 Ahau, 4 Ahau, 7 Ahau,

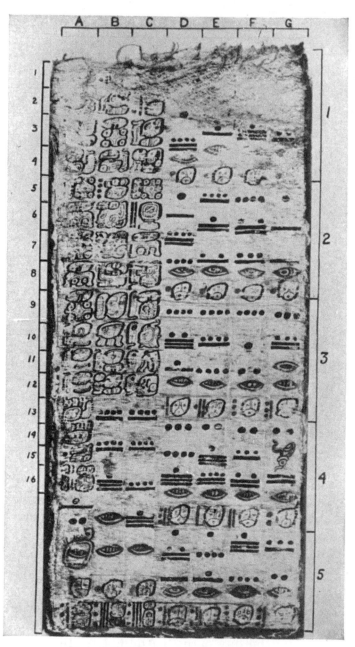

Plate XXIV. Page 24 Dresden Codex.

130

	A	B	C	D	E	F	G	
				1 1 1 14 0 1 Ahau	15 16 6 0 1 Ahau	10 10 16 0 1 Ahau	5 5 8 0 1 Ahau	1
		Hieroglyphs		1 5 14 4 0 1 Ahau	9 11 7 0 1 Ahau	4 12 8 0 1 Ahau	1 5 5 0 1 Ahau	2
				4 17 6 0 6 Ahau	4 9 4 0 11 Ahau	4 1 2 0 3 Ahau	3 13 0 0 8 Ahau	3
		9 9 16	9 9 9	3 4 16 0 13 Ahau	2 16 14 0 5 Ahau	2 8 12 0 10 Ahau	2 0 10 0 2 Ahau	4
	6 2 0 4 Ahau 8 Cumhu	0 0 0 1 Ahau 18 Kayab	16 0 0 1 Ahau 18 Uo	1 12 5 [8] 0 7 Ahau	1 4 6 0 12 Ahau	16 4 0 4 Ahau	8 2 0 9 Ahau	5

Diagram showing partial reduction of Mayan numbers into Arabic numbers in the calculation shown on page 24 of the Dresden Codex (Plate XXIV).

	A	B	C	D	E	F	G	
				151,840 1 Ahau	113,880 1 Ahau	75,920 1 Ahau	37,960 1 Ahau	1
		Hieroglyphs		185,120 1 Ahau	68,900 1 Ahau	33,280 1 Ahau	9,100 1 Ahau	2
				35,040 6 Ahau	32,120 11 Ahau	29,200 3 Ahau	26,280 8 Ahau	3
				23,360 13 Ahau	20,440 5 Ahau	17,520 10 Ahau	14,600 2 Ahau	4
	2,200 4 Ahau 8 Cumhu	1,366,560 1 Ahau 18 Kayab	1,364,360 1 Ahau 18 Uo	11,680 7 Ahau	8,760 12 Ahau	5,840 4 Ahau	2,920 9 Ahau	5

Diagram showing complete reduction into Arabic numbers of the calculation shown on page 24 of the Dresden Codex (Plate XXIV).

12 Ahau, etc., that fall at regular intervals of 2920 days.

From section 3, the calculation jumps to section 1 where the numbers in the original are partly destroyed. They have, however, been restored with perfect assurance since the days in all instances are 1 Ahau and therefore must be separated by multiples of 260 days. The number in G1 has been restored as 5-5-8-0 or 37,960 or 13 × 2920. It contains 260 an even number of times and therefore every successive period of 37,960 days begins with

Fig. 48. Mayan Ceremony as represented in the Dresden Codex. The figure at the left beats a drum while the one on the right plays a flageolet. The sound is indicated by scrolls. The head on the pyramid is that of the Maize God and it rests upon the sign *caban*, meaning earth.

the same day, 1 Ahau. It also equals 13 × 8 × 365 days or 104 years and 13 × 5 × 584 days or sixty-five revolutions of Venus.

The three numbers to the left in F1, E1, and D1 are respectively 2, 3, and 4 times 37,960. The last number, 151,840 days is therefore equal to 416 years or exactly 8 calendar rounds of 18,980 days.

The numbers in section 2 are more difficult to explain but they possibly have to do with corrections and correlations of astronomical periods. If we add to 1 Ahau 18 Kayab the number of days in E2, (68900), we arrive at a day 1 Ahau 13 Mac. This day is prominent in more detailed calculations elsewhere in the Dresden Codex. If we add to the same 1 Ahau 18 Kayab the number in D2 we arrive at 1 Ahau 18 Uo recorded at the bottom of C. Space permits no further explanation but the reader will see from the foregoing the method of experiment and cross checking that must be applied to the decipherment of the Mayan manuscripts. Fortunately, the relationships of numbers are absolute and the coincidences between the recorded numbers and astronomical periods are too close and frequent to be dismissed as accidental.

In addition to rational calculations dealing with astronomy one sees in the Mayan manuscripts many arrangements of the *tzolkin* supposed to bring to light good and bad days and to forecast events. A section of the Dresden Codex showing a condensed *tzolkin* is presented along with a diagram of its parts. At the top and right are seventeen hieroglyphs containing the symbols of the four directions, and of at least three of the principal gods. At the right is a column of five day signs with the number 3 at the head of the column. The permutation is divided into five parts of fifty-two days each and each part is subdivided into four groups of three days each. It begins with 3 Akbal, the day sign at the top of the column, and after the four subdivisions of thirteen days each have been counted we arrive at the day 3 Men, the second day sign in the column. The count is repeated till the

III	1 East	2 *	5 North	6 *	9 West	10 *	13 South
	3 God B	4 †	7 Woman	8 Good Days	11 God G	12 †	14 *
	13	III	13	III	13	III	15 God E

1 Akbal				16 Week of 13 days
2 Men				17 Ahau
3 Manik	God B—rain and sky god of good powers. Holds Kan (maize) sign in his hand.	Goddess with serpent headdress possibly connected with floods. Holds Kan sign in hand.	God K—benevolent sun god. If space had been larger God E (the maize god) would probably have been drawn next.	
4 Cauac				
				13

Plate XXV. (*a*) Detail of the Dresden Codex showing *Tzolkin* used in Divination; (*b*) Analysis of the above *Tzolkin*, according to Förstemann.

260 days have been exhausted and we come back again to 3 Akbal. In the diagram the red numbers of the codex are represented by Roman numerals and the black numbers by Arabic numerals. Since the count in this example begins with 3 and the addition is always 13, or exactly one round of numbers, the resultant days always have the number 3.

The three pictures of gods give us an inkling into the significance of this particular table of chances. All of the gods carry the *kan* or maize sign in their hands. The first god is the benevolent rain god and the third is the benevolent sun god. Between them is seated the malevolent goddess of floods with a serpent on her head. The maize god is not shown but his hieroglyph is given. This *tzolkin* probably deals with agriculture and may be an attempt to determine lucky days for planting.

Correlation with Christian Chronology. The day for day correlation rests broadly on the placing of the date on the Lintel of the Initial Series at Chichen Itza in the first occupation of that city according to the chronicles. More specifically it rests upon statements in Mayan and Spanish documents relating to the completion of tuns and katuns in the never-languishing day count. Also consideration must be given the so-called Year-Bearers, these being the first days of current years which furnish the designations for such years. Bishop Landa has a specimen Mayan year with its equivalent days in the Spanish calendar; this is the year 12 Kan corresponding to 1553–1554 A. D. and the day 12 Kan is found in the Long Count position 12.9.17.9.4, 12 Kan 2 Pop, July 26, 1553, Gregorian Calendar.

The Mayan Eras. The zero of the Mayan day count, reached by subtracting 12.9.17.9.4 or 1,799,-104 days from the position declared above, is shown to be October 14, 3373 B. C. in the backward projection of the Gregorian calendar. The Gregorian readings are preferable to the Julian because they preserve the actual times in the tropical year, but it is sometimes useful to use the days of the Julian Period which can always be found by adding 489384 to the Mayan number.

Now Mayan history does not reach back to the zero date which must be regarded as a theoretical beginning or Mundane Era. The earliest object with a contemporary date is the Tuxtla Statuette with May 16, 98 B. C. It appears, however, that the really historic beginning of the day count was 7.0.0.0.0, 10 Ahau 18 Zac, August 6, 613 B. C. The calendar of months was probably inaugurated in 580 B. C. when 0 Pop, New Year's day, coincided with the winter solstice. A third era, 9.0.0.0.0, 8 Ahau 13 Ceh, February 10, 176 A. D., is the one used in the Mayan chronicles.

Astronomical Checks on the Correlation. The first astronomical checks which develop from the correlation explained above are dates which reach the equinoxes, solstices, etc., further marked by special hieroglyphs which are to be explained as ideographs of these stations in the natural year. For instance the most emphatic date in the three famous temples of the Sun, the Cross, and the Foliated Cross at Palenque is one written 9.12.18.5.16, 2 Cib 14 Mol, September 23, 430 A. D., which coincides with the autumnal equinox. In connection with this repeated date we find two glyphs both of which are admirable ideographs of the equinox. One is Ahau, a face explained as that of the Lord of Day, but here half covered with starry eyes, and the other is the Kin or sun symbol, half darkened with cross-hatching. At Comitan a round number date exactly coinciding with the equinox has a variant of this second ideograph.

Other strong proofs concern Venus and the Moon. Hieroglyphs of these heavenly bodies are found in combination with dates and these later actually reach significant phases of the planets in question. For Venus the phase chosen is commonly the first appearance as Morningstar four days after inferior conjunction, or what is known as the heliacal rising. Records of the Moon are prominent when a new or full phase coincides with a round number in the day count.

Astronomical Observatories. One of the most interesting pieces of evidence in support of the correlation explained above has to do with a giant sun dial at Copan. Two stelæ stand on opposite sides of the valley establishing a line which runs about 9 degrees north of west. When observation is made from the eastern marker the sun sets behind the western stone two times during the course of a year, once shortly after the vernal equinox and once shortly before the autumnal equinox. Now the Mayan chronicles state that the calendarial New Year was ''counted in order'' during a certain Katun 13 Ahau which extended from 491 A. D. to 511 A. D. Altar U at Copan was observed to record two New Year's dates equaling April 9 in conjunction with another date, equaling September 2, 503 A. D., and falling in the required interval covered by Katun 13 Ahau. These dates were such as might be reached by just such a base line as exists at Copan and it was first believed that they were exactly reached by it. Careful reconsideration of

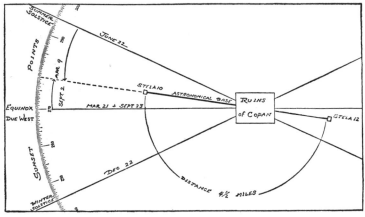

Fig. 49. Diagram of the Astronomical Base Line at Copan giving readings at April 9 and September 2. Slight shifts were made in this line: at an early time it was arranged to read April 5 and September 6 and at a later time April 12 and August 30.

the evidence in the inscriptions and a re-survey of the line of sight led to the interesting conclusion that the sun dial of Copan was originally set up in 392 A. D. to give sunset coincidences on April 5 and September 6. About 490 A. D. the stones were re-adjusted to give the April 9 and September 2 which are recorded on Altar U and still later a third and present arrangement was effected giving April 12 and August 30. Each pair of dates is "reciprocal" in the sense that one member marks the same interval after the Spring equinox that the other does before the Fall equinox. The shifting seems to have been decided upon by astronomical congresses, and the purpose was to fix propitious times of planting the crops.

Other Mayan observatories at Uaxactun and Chichen Itza have lines of sight which mark exactly the positions of the sun (the summer solstice, etc.), and all in all the evidence deduced from these observatories is in complete agreement with the correlation of the Mayan and Christian time counts originally effected on the evidence in sixteenth century documents.

The True Year. The base line at Copan yielded accurate data on the exact length of the tropical year, a period varying by a difficult fraction from 365 full days. The tropical year is the time measured by the revolution of the earth around the sun and by the recurring seasons. No agricultural people could neglect this natural time period with its obvious relation to planting and harvest.

Reference has already been made to the notational 360 day year (tun) of the Mayas and to their formal calendar year (haab) of exactly 365 days. The calendar year kept running ahead of the true year by the accumulating amount of the days which we intercalate on leap years but the Mayas wisely made no such intercalations since to have done so would have thrown their day count out of gear with the moon and other planets and the somewhat defective calendar based upon these minor heavenly bodies. Therefore the months of the Mayan year like those of the ancient Egyptian year slowly moved through the seasons. But the Mayas calculated an almost exact correction for the excess of the true year over the vague 365 day year. This excess amounts to about .24 of a day and their correction seems to have been one day in four years for short periods while for long periods they made 29 calendar rounds (1508 calendar years or 550,420 days) equal 1507 tropical years. This is a remarkably accurate adjustment, much closer, in fact, than that of our present Gregorian calendar. This great cycle is comparable to the 1460 year Sothic cycle of the Egyptians in so far as that relates to the flooding of the Nile, but the Egyptian arrangement has an error of about twelve days for the cycle while the Mayan arrangement is accurate to a very small fraction of a day.

In the calendars of various Guatemalan and Mexican tribes the slow shifting of the months is attested by actual statements of early Spanish writers. But the conventional 365 day year was, after all, sufficiently accurate for most purposes since associations between the months and the seasons would hold reasonably true for the average lifetime.

The Lunar Calendar. The apparent revolution of the moon around the earth was taken by the Mayas as the basis of a lunar calendar distinct from the civil calendar, but used in combination with it for various ceremonial purposes. Now the average duration of a lunar revolution is 29 days, 12 hours, 44 minutes, 2.87 seconds. Twelve lunations amount to a little more than 354 days and are therefore far short of a true year. Primitive peoples whose principal interest is to keep the moon in adjustment with the seasons have an occasional thirteenth month in their luni-solar calendars.

The Metonic cycle of the Greeks, an equation of 19 tropical years, 235 lunations and 6940 days, has been regarded as a remarkable achievement in observation. The Mayas discovered the same equation and with their system of designating days were able to use it with much greater ease than the Greeks since one katun minus one tzolkin gives exactly the required number of days:—

$$1. \ 0. \ 0.0 = 7200 \text{ days}$$
$$13.0 = \ 260 \text{ days}$$
$$19. \ 5.0 = 6940 \text{ days}$$

This interval is used prominently in several calculations at Copan and Quirigua.

On pages 51 to 58 of the Dresden Codex is found a remarkable lunar calendar covering 405 lunations or nearly 33 years. The lunar revolutions are arranged in groups of five or six, the former calculated at 148 days and the latter at 177 or 178 days. These are the necessary intervals between eclipses. The total amounts to 11,960 days which exactly contains the tzolkin and therefore forms a cycle. It is a remarkable fact that 405 lunar revolutions amount, according to modern calculations, to 11,959.888 or only 0.112 of a day less than the Mayan lunar calendar. Therefore this re entering series can be used nine times, or nearly 300 years, before an error amounting to one whole day has accumulated. There is also evidence that the Mayas used the great cycle of 29 × 52 calendar years, or 1507 tropical years, in connection with the moon and here the error for 18,639 lunations is about .64 of a day.

The Supplementary Series in Long Count dates is probably to be interpreted as the statement of the day reached by the Initial Series in a lunar calendar with an accumulated error; that is, the Mayas had an uncorrected lunar count as well as an uncorrected calendar year. Glyph C records a number of complete lunations which is never in excess of six; Glyph D gives the number of days in the current lunation when these are 19 or less and Glyph E, which has the basic value of 20, finishes the count

Fig. 50.   Representations of the Moon: *a*, sun and moon hieroglyphs; *b*, moon from a "celestial band"; *c*, moon hieroglyph used for 20 in codices.

of a current lunation.   There is some evidence that the Mayan lunar calendar in the fifth century A. D. had receded about four days from the true positions of the moon, the count being made from the new or conjunctional phase.   When, however, a new or full

Fig. 51.   The Last Glyph of the Supplementary Series: *a*, moon glyph; combined with the numeral 9 or 10 to indicate a 29 or a 30 day lunar month.

phase actually coincided with an important round number in the day count special record of the fact was made.

The lunar table in the Dresden Codex does not apply precisely to records of the First Empire but possibly may be adjusted to the times of the Second Empire.   The indications are, however, too complicated to be examined in detail.

Venus Calendar. Mayan astronomers reached a remarkable knowledge of the movements of the planet Venus and evolved a Venus calendar based essentially on the correspondence between 8 calendar years of 365 days each and 5 apparent or synodical revolutions of Venus of 584 days each. Venus whirling on an inside orbit actually makes thirteen revolutions around the sun in very nearly the same time that the earth makes eight revolutions and therefore passes between the earth and the sun five times (the difference between 13 and 8) during the course of this astronomical period of 2920 days. Just before inferior conjunction the planet disappears as evening star and a few days later emerges as morning star. The mean length of the synodical revolution of Venus is 583.92 days and the actual length may vary about four days from this mean. While the Mayas standardized the Earth year at 365 days and the Venus year at 584 days, they were fully aware of the amount of error in each case, and made proper correction for it without resorting to the devices of intercalation or excision.

We have seen that the Mayas manipulated the year and the lunation in combination with the tzolkin or permutation of 20 days and 13 numbers. They also found a round of these elements in combination with the phases of Venus. Since the period of 2920 days is divisible by 20 but not by 13 it had to be taken 13 times before the round of the Venus calendar was reached.

In the Dresden Codex five pages are devoted to this round of the Venus calendar. Each Venus year of 584 days is divided into four parts of 236 days for the phase of morning star, 90 days (superior conjunction), 250 days (evening star) and 8 days (inferior conjunction).   These divisions agree closely enough with actual appearance.   But we must remember that the observations were made without instruments and that the planet cannot be seen by the naked eye when close to the sun.   Moreover we must expect beliefs as to the nature of this planet, personified as a god, to supplement the knowledge gained from actual observations.   The obscuration of Venus at inferior conjunction seems to have been greatly dreaded especially when a round number in the day count fell within the eight days of its duration.   A grotesque two-headed monster apparently ruled this fatal period: on the front head is seen the symbol of Venus and on the rear head the symbol of the sun, both associated with elements of death.

The Venus calendar seems to have taken form in the sixth century B. C. on the basis of heliacal risings of the planet as morning star in sets of five making an eight year cycle.   The dates in the Mayan calendar especially emphasized in connection with Venus are 19 Xul, 18 Kayab, 12 Yax, 6 Zip, and 5 Kankin standing exactly 584 days apart, while the corresponding dates in the Gregorian calendar are April 12, November 17, June 24, January 29, and September 5.   When these sets of dates, one in a fixed and the other in a vague calendar are carried back to a common focus they are found to correspond very closely with the proper astronomical phase of Venus.   The maximum difference of the true positions of Venus from the positions in the Venus calendar is then only two days, plus or minus.

The coincidences of the 8 day period of obscuration of Venus at inferior conjunction with the following round numbers in the day count was memorialized by important monuments:—

9.14.0.0.0, 6 Ahau 13 Muan,   Feb. 4, 452 A. D. Venus rises as morning star

9.17.0.0.0, 13 Ahau 18 Cumhu, Mar. 27, 511 A. D. Venus invisible during conjunction

10. 0.0.0.0, 7 Ahau 18 Zip,   May 17, 570 A. D. Venus invisible during conjunction

10. 3.0.0.0, 1 Ahau 3 Yaxkin, July 6, 629 A. D. Venus about to set as evening star

The Venus table in the Dresden Codex, the introductory page of which has been explained in an earlier section (see Plate XXIV) emphasizes the same Mayan and Gregorian positions of Venus as the ancient monuments but this table was evidently intended to be used between the Tenth and Thirteenth centuries A. D. The point of departure for the table is 9.9.9.16.0, 1 Ahau 18 Kayab, April 12, 363 A. D., which does not coincide with an heliacal rising of the planet, although April 12 and 18 Kayab occur in other connections at the time of the inauguration of the Venus calendar in the Sixth century B. C. But in the Lunar table we find 10.19.6.1.0, 4 Ahau 18 Kayab, November 20, 950, which does reach an heliacal rising of Venus as morning star.

Summary of Mayan History. A brief summary of Mayan history is given below:—

PROTOHISTORIC PERIOD

613 B. C. to 176 A. D.   7.0.0.0.0 to 9.0.0.0.0

The counting of days apparently began on August 6, 613 B. C. and the civil calendar in perfected form was inaugurated about 580 B. C. when 0 Pop coincided with the winter solstice, while the Venus calendar emerged half a century later. The calendarial inventions, the numerical notation and the hieroglyphic system may, perhaps, be credited to the genius of one man afterwards deified as Itzamna. The earliest contemporary Mayan date occurs on a jade statuette from San Andres Tuxtla, and is May 16, 98 B. C. The next earliest one is on the jade tablet known as the Leyden Plate and is November 17, 60 A. D., having reference to the Venus calendar. This is followed almost immediately by several contemporary dates on monuments at Uaxactun which also are of astronomical import. The design on the Leyden Plate shows that the characteristic details of Mayan drawing had already been developed and we may surmise that during the protohistoric period the early carvings were on wood instead of stone and that the peculiar religion of the Mayas was even then beginning to crystallize around the serpent, the jaguar, etc.

EARLY PERIOD

176 A. D. to 373 A. D.   9.0.0.0.0 to 9.10.0.0.0

During these ten katuns the great cities of the south make rapid strides towards grandeur. Pyramidal mounds are erected and temples built upon them. Public squares are laid out and in these are set up stelæ and altars. The leading early cities are Palenque, Tikal, and Copan, where the dated monuments and temples mark rapid progress in the arts of sculpture and architecture while the subject matter of inscriptions reveals growing ability in astronomy and mathematics. Low angular relief characterizes stone sculptures and the profile presentation of the human figure is now handled more skilfully than front view.

MIDDLE PERIOD

373 A. D. to 471 A. D.   9.10.0.0.0 to 9.15.0.0.0

Some of the most beautiful monuments of the Mayas belong to this middle period. While archaism does not entirely disappear there is freshness, purity of style, and straightforwardness of presentation about the sculpture of this age. Flamboyancy is not apparent. At Copan the Great Mound was practically carried to completion during this period, an enormous undertaking which absorbed so much energy that few stelæ were set up. The best series of monuments from the middle period are seen at Naranjo and Piedras Negras.

GREAT PERIOD

471 A. D. to 629 A. D.   9.15.0.0.0 to 10.3.0.0.0

Many cities flourished in the culminating years of Mayan civilization. In addition to those already mentioned Quirigua, Ixkun, Seibal, Nakum, Cancuen, Yaxchilan, Toniná, and Kobá were important centers while a complete list of the sites with dated monuments would show many more names. The territorial extension reaches from northern Yucatan to the Guatemalan highlands and from southern Vera Cruz to central Honduras. Art passes through interesting changes with tendencies towards flamboyancy. Architecture makes great advances: rooms become wider, walls thinner and forms more refined and pleasing. The calculations deal more and more with complicated astronomical subjects and dates belong less and less in the category of contemporary history. The first age of Mayan civilization, called the First Empire, comes to an end with Katun 3 of Cycle 10, a date registered at Uaxactun which, strangely enough, also boasts the earliest stela with a contemporary date. It is indicated that Uaxactun was occupied for 561 years while the range of dates at Tikal is 394 years. Abandonment of all the sites of the First Empire took place within something like fifty years. What caused this collapse? Civil war? Social decadence? Failure of food supply? Or perhaps some overwhelming epidemic? There is good reason for believing that the sudden appearance of yellow fever may have had a part in the catastrophe. References in the Chronicles to the First Empire are very brief and do not help us find the answer to this mystery.

TRANSITION PERIOD

629 A. D. to 964 A. D.   10.3.0.0.0 to 11.0.0.0.0

Most of the Mayas surviving the collapse of the First Empire seem to have found a second home in western Yucatan, especially in the region called Chakunputun in the Chronicles. Here the rainfall is much less and the forest environment not nearly so luxuriant. Certain cities, which probably date from this transitional period, such as Hochob, Dzibilnocac, Rio Bec, etc., have very beautiful architecture showing advances over that of the First Empire in some features. Dated documents are so rare as practically to be non-existent. It seems probable that Mayan learning had been reduced to books for there is ample evidence from the succeeding period that astronomical and calendarial knowledge had been conserved from ancient times. At the end of these lean centuries, the Mayas made their way still farther north. Chichen Itza which had been a provincial city of the First Empire was reoccupied and the Mayan renaissance known as the Second Empire began.

PERIOD OF THE LEAGUE OF MAYAPAN

964 A. D. to 1191 A. D.   11.0.0.0.0 to 11.11.10.0.0

The first phase of the Mayan renaissance was pretty clearly centered in Chichen Itza although the earliest date which may be contemporary is probably that of the Temple of the Initial Series at Holactun. The inscription shows a survival of the ancient method of counting time and is now believed to treat of the interval between March 9, 1012 A. D. and November 14, 1016 A. D. Other cities rising to splendor during the Second Empire are Kabah, Labna, Sayil, and Izamal. The time of foundation for Uxmal is rather difficult to determine. According to tradition it was the capital of Toltec immigrants into Yucatan, but when or how they arrived cannot be answered definitely. The League of Mayapan was organized as an alliance between Chichen Itza and Uxmal in the second half of the twelfth century, and Mayapan was built as a neutralized capital of church and state under the inspiration of a Toltec noble named Quetzalcoatl. Finally, Izamal and Chichen Itza rebelled and Inetzalcoatl conquered the latter city in 1191 and made it the capital of a Maya-Toltec state.

PERIOD OF MEXICAN INFLUENCE

1191 A. D. to 1437 A. D.   11.11.10.0.0 to 12.4.0.0.0

The helpers of Hunac Ceel bore Mexican names and belonged to the Toltec nation. Hunac Ceel is identified in one place with Kukulcan, the name meaning "plumed serpent" in the Mayan language, and in another place with Quetzalcoatl which has the same significance in the Mexican language. In Chichen Itza sculptural art and architecture have many clear analogies to works in the Valley of Mexico. The building called the Castillo seems to have been built by Quetzalcoatl, being the first structure in which serpent columns and other structural ideas of this ruler were given expression. The Temple of the High Priest's Grave is a developed example of the new style bearing the date December 31, 1339 A. D. The elaborate Group of the Columns with the famous Temple of the Warriors, may be still later.

In the first half of the fifteenth century civil war and epidemic disease brought about a second depopulation of the stone-built cities including Chichen Itza, Mayapan, Uxmal, and probably also numerous other sites in the region of Uxmal. The last monument at Mayapan may declare the date September 28, 1437.

MODERN PERIOD

1437 A. D. to the present day.

After the second general abandonment of urban life the Mayas seem to have been divided into many warring factions. Temples were still regarded as sacred and some constructions in stone and mortar were still made, as we know from the first Spanish descriptions of towns on the east coast of Yucatan. Tulum probably represented this last phase and this site on a cliff overlooking the Caribbean is probably the city compared to Seville by the coasting expedition of Grijalva in 1518. A monument at

Tulum is believed to record the last setting up of a katun stone by the Mayas on 12.8.0.0.0, 2 Ahau 3 Pop, August 5, 1516, almost exactly 2129 years after the Mayas began to count every day in order.

At the present time certain ancient ideas still persist among the Lacandone Indians of the lowlands and among the Quiché, Cakchiquels, and several other tribes of the highlands. But the old glory of the Mayan civilizations has passed away never to return. A prophetic vision of this end is found in one of the Mayan Books of Chilam Balam which relates to events immediately after the founding of Merida.

"It was then that the teaching of Christianity began, that shall be universal over our land. Then began the construction of the church here in the center of the town of Tihoo: great labor was the destiny of the katun. Then began the execution by hanging, and the fire at the ends of our hands. Then also came ropes and cords into the world. Then the children of the younger brothers (the Indians) passed under the hardship of legal summons and tribute. Tribute was introduced on a large scale and Christianity was introduced on a large scale. Then the seven sacraments of the word of God were established. Let us receive our guests heartily: our elder brothers (the white men) come!"

Plate XXVI. General View of Monte Alban from the North. The mounds are arranged around courts in an orderly manner.

CHAPTER III

THE MIDDLE CIVILIZATIONS

THE influence of the Mayan civilization when at its height (400 to 600 A. D.) may be traced far beyond the limits of the Mayan area. Ideas in art, religion, and government that were then spread broadcast served to quicken nations of diverse speech and a series of divergent cultures resulted. Most of these lesser civilizations were at their best long after the great Mayan civilization had declined, but one or two were possibly contemporary. It will be the aim in the present chapter to emphasize the indebtedness of these lesser civilizations to the Mayas as well as to comment upon their individual characters.

We will first proceed northwest into Mexico and then southeast into the Isthmus of Panama. The environment under which the Mayas developed their arts of life continues in narrowing bands westward along the Gulf of Mexico and southward across the Isthmus of Tehuantepec. The most westerly Mayan city of importance seems to have been Comalcalco. But there is also a large ruin near San Andres Tuxtla and it may be significant that the earliest dated object of the Mayas (the Tuxtla Statuette) came from this region. In other words, the cradle of Mayan culture may have been in this coastal belt where arid and humid conditions exist side by side and where the figurines of the archaic type are found together with those of the Mayas. Unfortunately, the archæology of this part of Mexico has been little studied.

153

The Olmeca or Rubber People. The Olmeca may be placed in the humid region of southern Vera Cruz and western Tabasco which the Aztecs of later times called Nonoalco. This region is frequently mentioned in the most ancient of the Mexican traditions, doubtless symbolizing in a general way the civilizing contacts with the Mayas. Rubber is called *olli* in the Mexican language and while the earliest known specimens of rubber are those found in the Sacred Cenote at Chichen Itza, the ceremonial and practical uses of the material are mostly mentioned in connection with the Olmeca and Totonac peoples. Rubber was used for incense, for water-proofing purposes, to tip drumsticks, etc. A large rubber ball was also used in a sacred game which may be compared to basket ball since the goals were rings set high up in the parallel walls of a specially constructed court.

According to Ixtlilxochitl's history the Olmeca came before the Toltecs and were the first to extend their civilizing rule over parts of the Mexican highlands. Some authorities think the Olmeca were a Mayan tribe but it is quite possible that they spoke Mexican. They may have fled south at the breakdown of the Toltec empire for we find in Nicaragua at the time of the Conquest a group of this name with traditions pointing to the far north. The ruins found in 1927 by the writer at Cerro de las Mesas, west of Alvarado Lagoon, may possibly be ascribed to this people. The site contains seventeen monuments, several of which are dedicated to Quetzalcoatl and must be referred to the thirteenth century. Bars and dots are used in connection with day signs to record dates which may belong to the

Plate XXVII. Detail of Monte Alban showing Wall Foundations and Small Cell-like Rooms.

155

calendarial system appearing on Zapotecan monuments.

Zapotecan Culture.   In the State of Oaxaca the Zapotecan Indians attained to a high degree of civilization, but a study of their culture shows they were profoundly indebted to the Mayas for many ideas.   Monte Alban, the White Mountain, overlooking the modern City of Oaxaca is the principal archæological site in point of size and may have been the ancient capital.   It was abandoned before the coming of the Spaniards, however, and Mitla appears to have taken its place.

Fig. 52.   Comparison of Mayan and Zapotecan Serpent Heads. The first two examples are from Palenque and the second two from Monte Alban.

Unfortunately no extensive traditions have come down to us to help in the restoration of Zapotecan history, or in that of the neighboring Mixtecs.   Although the art, hieroglyphic writing, and calendar system were pretty clearly derived from the Mayas, nevertheless there was time and opportunity for these to develop interesting characters of their own. It is impossible to tell from the record whether the Zapotecs ever embarked on a career of empire: the area in which the full complex of the characteristic products occurs is practically limited to the area at present occupied by the tribe.   It is quite possible that the Zapotecs were conquered by the Toltecs in the twelfth century and that such similarities as exist between the forms of Zapotecan sculptural art and those of the Toltec cities of Xochicalco and Teotihuacan in central Mexico, on the one hand, and those of Pipil and Chorotegan sites in Guatemala and Salvador, on the other hand, are to be explained by intercommunications under the Toltec régime.

Fig. 53.   Bar and Dot Numerals combined with Hieroglyphs on Zapotecan Monuments.

Monte Alban and Mitla stand in strong contrast to each other, the first crowning a mountain ridge, the second occupying a valley site.   Monte Alban has no buildings intact, but shows a vast assemblage of enormous pyramids and platforms.   Mitla has only one small pyramid, but boasts a series of finely preserved temples on low platform bases.   In Monte Alban we find monolithic monuments comparable to the stelæ of the Mayas, and carrying hieroglyphic inscriptions: also pottery figurines and jade amulets in a style which follows rather closely the models developed in the early cities of the humid lowlands.   At Mitla there are none of these things: instead, the architectural decoration shows a most interesting use of textile designs treated in a mosaic of cut stones.   It is apparent then that a long record of high culture is to be found in the Zapotecan field.

At Monte Alban there are one or two narrow vaulted chambers in mounds, but on the tops of the mounds the few excavations have disclosed only

Plate XXVIII. Zapotecan Art: Incense Burners, Funerary Vases of Portrait Type, Cruciform Tomb with Geometric Decoration.

simple cell-like rooms which probably had flat roofs. Some hints of ancient architectural decoration can be picked up here and there. Figures similar to those modeled in bold relief on the fronts of the cylindrical funeral urns (see frontispiece) seem to have been used over doorways, somewhat after the fashion of the Mayan mask panels.

The hieroglyphs that are found on the stelæ of Monte Alban and on stone slabs from other sites, resemble the Mayan hieroglyphs in the use of bar and dot numerals, but the day and month signs have never been identified with either the Mayan or Aztecan system, although almost certainly dealing with the same type of calendar. Lintels with lines of hieroglyphs on the outer edge have been found in burial chambers at Cuilapa and Xoxo. The forms at the former site are clearly and beautifully drawn, while at the latter site they are degenerate and probably merely decorative.

In Zapotecan funerary urns a close connection with Mayan art can easily be demonstrated. The urns are cylindrical vessels concealed behind elaborate figures built up from moulded and modeled pieces. Many of these built-up figures clearly represent human beings while others represent grotesque divinities or human beings wearing the masks of divinities. The purely human types have a formal modeling in high relief, the head usually being out of proportion to the rest of the body. The pose is ordinarily a seated one with the hands resting on the knees or folded over the breast. Details of dress are very clearly shown including capes, girdles, aprons, or skirts and headdresses. Necklaces are often worn with a crossbar pendant to which shells are attached. Headdresses are made of feathers and grotesque faces and are often very elaborate. As for the divine types the jaguar and a long-nosed reptile are the most common. The latter has a human body and may possibly be an adaptation of the Mayan Long-nosed God.

The funerary urns are found in burial mounds called *mogotes* which contain cell-like burial chambers. The urns are not found within these cells but on the floor in front of them, in a niche over the door, or even on the roof. They are frequently encountered in groups of five and seem never to contain offerings.

Other Zapotecan pottery is mostly made of the same bluish clay used in the urns. This clay is finely adapted to plastic treatment but never carries painted designs. The pottery products include pitchers of beautiful and unusual shapes, dishes with tripod legs modeled into serpent heads, incense burners, bowls, plates, etc. Of the same clay are also made whistles in realistic forms, and moulded figurines. Painted pottery also occurs in forms and designs of rare beauty, but it is much less characteristic of the Zapotecan province than the unpainted ware.

Carved jades of splendid workmanship have been recovered in the Zapotecan region and there is reason to believe that this semi-precious stone was obtained here in the natural state. Many of the pieces are smoothed only on the front, while the back retains its old weathered and stream-worn surface. Beautiful examples of gold work found in this region must be given a late date.

Splendid manuscripts were obtained by the Spaniards in the Zapotecan region, but the pictures of the gods as well as the hieroglyphs show strong

Aztecan influences. These
will be discussed briefly in
a later section. Some ac-
counts have been preserved
of the special features of
Zapotecan religion which
mark them off rather
sharply from the Aztecs,
however.

The high priests of the
Zapotecans were called
"Seers" and the ordinary
priests were "Guardians
of the Gods" and "Sacri-
ficers." There was a sort
of priestly college where
the sons of chiefs were
trained in the service of
the gods. The religious
practices included incense
burning, sacrificing of
birds, and animals, and let-
ting of one's own blood by
piercing the tongue and the
ear. Human sacrifice was
made on stated occasions
and was attended by rites
of great solemnity. The
Zapotecs never went to the
blood excesses that stain
the annals of the Aztecs.

The 260 day cycle of the
time count, was subdivided
into four periods of 65
days and each period was

Fig. 54. Detail of Wall
Construction at Mitla, showing
the separately Carved Stones.

[a]

[b]

Plate XXIX. (a) Stone Sculpture of the Early Zapotecan Period showing Rulers seated upon Thrones before an Altar; (b) Jade Tablets pierced for Suspension, found in Zapotecan Tomb.

under control of a single god and was associated
with one of the cardinal points. Each period of
sixty-five days was further divided into five groups
of thirteen days for a ceremonial reason. Some
authorities have considered that the general form
of the Central American calendar originated in the
region of the Isthmus of Tehuantepec and spread
to the north and to the south. But dependable history in the Mayan area goes back much farther than
in the Zapotecan region and renders such a guess
extremely hazardous.

Mitla. The famous temples of Mitla are the best-
preserved examples of architecture on the highlands
of Mexico and are peculiar in form and decoration.
The word Mitla is a corruption of the Aztecan word

Fig. 55. Wall Paintings of Mitla, resembling in style the Pictographic Art of the Codices from Southern Mexico.

Mictlan, place of the dead. This site was the burial
ground of Zapotecan kings and may have been a
place of pilgrimage. It was conquered by the Aztecs in the last decade of the fifteenth century.
While the architecture belongs in a class by itself
the frescoes have the distinct character of the Aztecan period.

The remains at this site have already been con-
trasted with those at Monte Alban. There is one
fairly large mound at Mitla but it has no surviving

superstructure. The temples are placed on low platforms which usually contain cruciform tombs. The buildings are carefully oriented and are assembled in groups of four which almost enclose square paved courts. The heavy walls have surfaces of cut stone and a filling of concrete or rubble and are ornamented with longitudinal panels of geometric designs arranged according to a carefully worked out plan. The geometric patterns are based on textile art and the mosaics of separately carved stones which fit neatly together preserve for us the ancient designs on belts and mantles. The chambers are long and narrow and formerly had flat roofs which have completely vanished. The wide doorways usually have two piers which help to support the lintel blocks. These are carefully trimmed stones of great length and weight. All the outer surfaces of the Mitla temples were sized with plaster and painted red and the frescoes, traces of which can still be seen in several buildings, are in red and black upon a white base. Various gods and ceremonies are represented in these frescoes, but only the upper portion of the bands can be made out in detail.

Cruciform tombs are found under several of the temples at Mitla as well as at a number of neighboring sites such as Xaaga and Guiaroo. In these tombs the designs in panels appear on the inside and are carved directly on large blocks of stone. Pottery remains are rare in the cruciform tombs of the Mitla type but a few examples of gold work have been discovered in them.

Within a short distance of Mitla is a fortified hill with several heavy walls that still stand to the height of perhaps twenty feet. In the flat valley between this hill and the ruins a considerable number of potsherds are plowed up in the field.

Totonacan Culture. In the central part of the state of Vera Cruz are found the remains commonly referred to the Totonacan Indians. These Indians are southern neighbors of the Huastecas who are an outlying Mayan tribe. The Totonacan language

Fig. 50. The Eyes of Totonacan Figurines.

is according to some authorities thrown into the Mayan stock. If not truly Mayan it contains many loan words. This apparent connection in language is all the more interesting in view of the character of Totonacan art which also shows a strong strain of Mayan feeling and technique in certain products but an unmistakable likeness to the archaic art of the Mexican highlands in certain other products. The pottery faces in the archaic style are advanced beyond the average of such work and probably represent a late phase.

A series of eyes showing Totonacan modifications of the styles prevalent on the archaic pottery heads of the Highlands is given in Fig. 56. In some cases we find the simple single or double groove eyes and in other cases these eyes are made more conspicuous by the use of black bituminous paint. The eyeball is developed at the end of the series.

The smiling or laughing faces have a much higher technique and are perhaps the finest examples of clay modeling from the New World. These heads have tubular extensions at the back and were possibly set into temple walls. The faces and foreheads are broadened in accordance with the esthetic type of a forehead flattening people. While the faces vary so much in minor details as to create the impression that they are portraits of actual persons

Plate XXX. Laughing Head of the Totonacs, remarkable example of Freehand Modeling in Clay. Heads of this type probably served as decorative details on temple fronts.

they are alike in method of modeling. Nearly all are laughing or smiling in a very contagious fashion. Sometimes the tip of the tongue is caught between the teeth, sometimes the corners of the mouth are pulled down as if the smile were reluctant, and there are other individual variations in the expressions of lively and unrestrained mirth.

Perhaps the most famous objects found in Totonacan territory are the so-called "stone collars" or "sacrificial yokes." In size and shape these resemble horse collars, but in contrast to somewhat similar objects from Porto Rico they are usually open while the latter are closed. Nothing is really known concerning their use but there has been no lack of fanciful surmises. The most popular explanation is that the yokes were placed over the necks of victims about to be sacrificed. It is evident that the yokes were intended to be placed in a horizontal position because there is a plain lower surface and the ends are frequently carved with faces that are right side up only when the plain side is down. These yokes represent the richest and most elaborate works of art in the entire region since they are carved in the most finished manner from single blocks of exceedingly hard stone.

Other peculiarly shaped stones are found in the Totonacan area and are carved according to the same splendid technique. The "paddle-shaped" stones have been found in considerable numbers and their use, like that of the stone yokes, is absolutely unknown. It is evident from the carving that they were intended to be stood on end.

The designs on the sacrificial yokes and paddle stones are largely reptilian, but there are examples where the turkey, the coyote, as well as the human motive are treated somewhat after the manner of the Mayas. Plumed serpents, monkeys, centipedes, and crocodiles are interestingly drawn on pottery. An important site is Papantla where a remarkably

Plate XXXI. (a) An Elaborately Carved Stone Collar, an Example of the Best Sculpture of the Totonacan Indians; (b) A Palmate Stone from the State of Vera Cruz. Two grotesque figures are holding snakes in their mouths.

ornate pyramid rising in six terraces may be seen, as well as massive sculptures in the same style as the works of art described above. The front wall of each terrace on all four sides of the pyramid, except for the space occupied by the stairway, is divided into a series of niches neatly made of cut stone. Formerly each of these niches may have served to shelter the statue of some god. Many fine remains of Totonacan art have been recovered from the Island of Sacrifices in the harbor of Vera Cruz. This island retained its ancient sacrificial character in the time of the Spanish conquerors. It is apparent, however, that the culture had already changed greatly if we may judge by the ruins of Cempoalan, the Totonacan capital in the sixteenth century. The art of this city is largely Aztecan.

The Toltecs. Mexican history is greatly concerned with the Toltecs, the name meaning People of Tula, or Tollan, "place of the reeds." Evidence is accumulating that this Tula was not the comparatively insignificant ruin on the northern edge of the Valley of Mexico, but instead was the great city of San Juan Teotihuacan. The lesser Tula may have been founded about 1200 A. D., just before the collapse of Toltec power.

Archæology tells a more detailed and convincing story of the Toltecs than does recorded history. In the stratified remains at Atzcapotzalco, the objects accredited to the Toltecs overlie those of the first potters of the Archaic Period and are in striking contrast to them. The principal motives of Toltec decorative art are obviously related to the earlier more brilliant work of the Mayas. The pyramids of the Toltecs exceed in size those of the Mayas but are of inferior construction, adobe bricks with concrete facing taking the place of rubble and cut stone. The temples that crowned these pyramids were also of less solid construction and no single example is now intact. Vaulted ceilings were replaced by flat timbered ceilings or high pitched roofs of thatch. Sometimes in wide rooms columns were used as additional support for roof beams. The groundplans of buildings other than temples show small rooms arranged in an irregular fashion round courts.

The ceremonial game of *tlachtli* resembling basket ball was an important feature of Toltec religion. It may have been obtained from the Olmeca, but at any rate spread far and wide under the Toltec régime. Another feature of Toltec religion was the worship of the sun's disk which is reflected in various sculptures. Also this people are supposed to have invented *pulque,* made from the fermented sap of the agave. The reclining type of sculpture known as Chacmool, after the famous example found at Chichen Itza in northern Yucatan, may be a relic of a peculiar Toltec cult in which drunkenness figured. Human sacrifice was another feature of the religion of the Mexican highlands in contrast to that of the lowland Mayas. On the economic side Toltec culture rested on the earlier Archaic civilization, but on the artistic and ceremonial side it was largely inspired by the Mayas through the mediation of the Zapotecs, Olmecs, and Totonacs, but with new emphasis on certain aspects and several important innovations. The language of the Toltecs seems to have been essentially the same as that of the Aztecs who succeeded them.

The Toltecs made a radical departure in social policy in that they took to war and expropriation as a means of building up national wealth, thereby paralleling, somewhat ineffectively to be sure, the political methods of Europe and Western Asia. There had been war before their time in Central America, but not apparently for aggrandizement. The Mayas, and most other Mexican and Central American nations, developed excess food supply which released many persons for the pursuit of art and science. Perhaps it was pressure of population upon food supply in an arid land that directed the Toltecs towards tribute taking. At least the fact is reasonably clear that this people did embark upon a short-lived career of conquest and that they levied tribute of precious stones and precious metals and secured by the same means an augmented food supply.

There is confusion and reduplication in the lists of Toltec rulers and only three great names in succession can be regarded as certain. These are Huetzin, Ihuitimal, and Quetzalcoatl, although it seems probable that there was a still earlier chieftain named Mixcoatl or Mixcoamazatl and that two successors of Quetzalcoatl were Matlaxochitl and Nauyotl, the last-named also figuring as the first lord of Colhuacan. Then follow various dynastic lists for several Mexican tribes which flourished between the downfall of the Toltecs and the coming of the Spaniards.

Quetzalcoatl and the Toltec Era. The chronology of the Toltecs and their successors is greatly dilated in several historical compilations made after the Spanish conquest by intelligent natives who interpreted fragments of ancient pictographic year counts then surviving in Mexico. Thanks to a mod-crn survey of materials much more extensive than those which Chimalpahin, Ixtlilxochitl, etc., had at their disposal, we are now able to avoid the errors of these writers.

In the original pre-Spanish chronicles important events are recorded in connection with fifty-two year signs falling in regular order and then repeating. In the well-intentioned attempts to restore Mexican history entire cycles are interpolated in several places and the rulers are given lives of impossible length. In the case of Ixtlilxochitl we possess, fortunately, the principal documents which this descendant of the Texcocan kings attempted to interpret. Also in the case of the Annals of Quauhtitlan, an early compilation made by a nameless student of ancient history, we are in position to adjudicate wide errors in chronology. There is an annotation on this manuscript reading "6 times 4 centuries, plus 1 century, plus 13 years, today the 22nd of May 1558." The "centuries" are the native cycles of fifty-two years and the total on this basis would amount to 1313 years. Subtracted from 1558 the beginning would be found in 245 A. D., while the years set down by the compiler in an unbroken series reach back to 635 A. D. But there is no pre-Spanish support for written history, outside the Mayan area, of anything like this antiquity.

The Toltec Era was established by Quetzalcoatl, after a simplified model of the Mayan calendar, on August 6, 1168 A. D., this date corresponding to a day 1 Tecpatl (1 Flint) in the first position of a month Toxcatl. This day gave its name to the entire year and its hieroglyph was one of a series of fifty-two used to designate years in the pictographic

records. Most of the Mexican year counts begin
with the particular sign 1 Tecpatl which corresponds
to 1168–69 A. D. In others there is reference to a
day 7 Acatl 1 Panquetzaliztli in a year 2 Acatl (February 16, 1195 A. D.) upon which a new fire ceremony, established by Quetzalcoatl in accordance
with Mayan usage, was celebrated at intervals of
fifty-two years.

The conclusions are supported by evidence in
Guatemalan chronicles and also in records of the
Mayas for we have already seen that Quetzalcoatl
conquered Chichen Itza in 1191 A. D. The three
great Toltec emperors, Huetzin, Ihuitimal, and
Quetzalcoatl, swept over an area extending from
Durango to Nicaragua, the three seats of their gov-
ernment being Teotihuacan in the Valley of Mexico,
Chichen Itza in Yucatan, and Iximché in Guatemala.

Quetzalcoatl probably spent his youth in Yucatan,
returning to his highland home with strange religious and social ideas. His opposition to the Toltec
idea of human sacrifice was followed by a war of
cults. Quetzalcoatl began the construction at Tula
with serpent columns like those of his lofty temple
in Chichen Itza. Also he appears to have founded
Cholula as a special center for his humane religion.
His death occurred in connection with a prognosti-
cation in the Venus calendar of the Mayas, for the
year 1 Acatl, 1207–08 A. D.

Quetzalcoatl, perhaps the most remarkable figure
in ancient American history, was emperor, artist,
scientist, and humanist philosopher. He established orders of knighthood as well as the corona-
tion ceremony used by the later Mexican kings. He
developed the various industrial arts and built up
a wide trade in cotton, cacao, and other products.

Plate XXXII. The Temple at Xochicalco before Restoration. The lower part of the picture shows the sculptured base of the temple pyramid. The walls of the temple itself are seen above.

As a patron of the peripatetic merchant he appears under the name Nacxitl, which means Four-way Foot. Apotheosis being an idea strongly fixed among the Toltecs, Quetzalcoatl was deified as Ehecatl, God of Winds, on account of his support of the Mayan god of rainstorms, and for his astronomical work he was further deified as God of the Planet Venus.

San Juan Teotihuacan. This name Teotihuacan means Where the Gods (i.e., the deified dead) Dwell. This enormous ruin is located on the eastern margin of the Valley of Mexico. The principal features of Teotihuacan are two great pyramids and a straight roadway lined with small pyramids. There are also several groups of buildings of which the lower walls and the bases of the piers are still to be seen as well as some interesting fragments of fresco painting. The smaller of the two great pyramids is called the Pyramid of the Moon. It is located at the end of the roadway which is commonly called the Pathway of the Dead. The Pyramid of the Sun is situated on the east side of the roadway. This pyramid is about 180 feet in height and rises in four sloping terraces. The temple which formerly crowned its summit has entirely disappeared. Explorations conducted by the Mexican government showed that this pyramid was enlarged from time to time and old stairways buried under new masonry. On the south side of the small stream that flows through the ruins is a group of buildings called the Citadel.

In 1921 the Mexican Government undertook a restoration of the Citadel, following the discovery of remarkable sculptures on the principal pyramid. It appears that in ancient times this pyramid was

[a]

[b]

Plate XXXIII. Two Views of the Principal Pyramid in the Citadel at Teotihuacan. (a) General view of the original mass of the pyramid at the back with the reconstructed addition in front. (b) View of stairway and various walls covered up and preserved by the addition.

176

enlarged by an addition to one side and the richly ornamented terraces and stairway buried (Plate XXXIII). The sculptured stones from the other three sides of the temple were allowed to fall into neglect by the Toltecs or were carried away and put to other uses, but the portion buried was kept in its original state. The colors are still bright in many places and the great heads of plumed serpents and obsidian butterflies sometimes retain their inset eyes of obsidian. The decoration is a repeated motive. The head of the feathered serpent projects outward from the terrace walls and from the balustrade of the stairway, while the body is in low relief. The tail of the serpent has a rattle, and the body is covered with feathers. Shells are seen below the serpent where the body arches and just in front of the tail is a massive head with two rings on the frontal. This doubtless represents the Obsidian Butterfly, a divinity of great importance among the Toltecs, which is represented unmistakably in frescoes at Teotihuacan as well as on pottery. The Citadel well deserves its name, since it is a great enclosure, much like a fort, with buildings upon its bulwarks, and with steep outer walls, which could easily be defended.

A few large sculptures have been found at Teotihuacan. But the site is chiefly remarkable for pottery figurines and heads that are picked up by thousands. The heads present such a marked variety of facial contour and expression that it would seem as if every race under the sun had served as models. It is very likely that these heads formed part of votive offerings, being attached to bodies made of some perishable material. The heads were seldom used to adorn pottery vessels, although many mod-

ern and fraudulent vases are so adorned. Dolls
with head and torso in one piece and with movable
arms and legs made of separate pieces were known.
The face of Tlaloc, the Rain God, is fairly common
in Teotihuacan pottery but other deities have not
surely been identified. It is not improbable that
the God of Fire is personified as an old man with

wrinkled face, but somewhat less
likely that Xipe is represented in
the faces that look out through
the three holes of a mask. The
jaguar, the monkey, the owl, and
other animals are also modeled
with excellent fidelity. The
Mayan convention of the human
face in the open jaws of the serpent is not unknown.

A number of beautiful vases
painted in soft greens, pinks, and
yellows have been recovered
at Teotihuacan. These colors
would not stand the kiln and
they were applied after the vessel had been burned. According
to one method, the outside of the
vessel was covered with a fine
coating of plaster upon which

Fig. 57.   Jointed
Doll of Clay from San
Juan Teotihuacan.

the design was painted exactly as in fresco. According to a second method the effect of *cloisonné*
was cleverly achieved. This technique is most characteristic of the region northwest of the Valley of
Mexico and will be described later. Incised or engraved designs are commonly met with on pottery
vessels at Teotihuacan. No inscriptions have been

found at this ruin, in spite of the many years of exploration.

Xochicalco. Let us now pass over in brief review several ruins which belong to the Toltecan period. Xochicalco, the House of the Flowers, is a large ruin near Cuernavaca. The position seems to have been chosen primarily for defense. The rounded ridge that drops off into deep valleys on either side is laid out in courts, terraces, and pyramids. Only one building offers evidence of the sculptural skill of the ancient habitants. It is a temple, standing upon a rather low platform mound. The sides of the platform mound are decorated with great plumed serpents, seated human figures, hieroglyphs, etc. Parts of the sculptures also remain on the low walls of the temple itself which is now roofless. The stone carving at Xochicalco resembles that of Monte Alban especially as regards the hieroglyphs and is probably of somewhat later date than Teotihuacan. All in all the conclusion seems safe that writing was unknown outside the Mayan area before Quetzal-coatl devised ways and means.

Tula. Building stone of good quality was available at this site and in consequence sculptures are plentiful. Particularly famous are the great sculptured columns which represent feathered serpents and gigantic human figures. The drums are mostly mortised and the columns are crowned by true capitals. These architectural features at Tula find their closest counterpart at the Mayan city of Chichen Itza in northern Yucatan. The *tlachtli* or ball court occurs at Tula and the groundplans of complicated "palaces" can also be made out.

Cholula. The sacred city of Cholula, in the environs at Puebla, is chiefly famous for its great pyramid. This structure is more or less irregular in shape but the base averages more than a thousand feet on the side and the total height, now somewhat reduced, was probably close to two hundred feet above the plain. Compared with the Pyramid of Cheops, it covers nearly twice as much ground and has a much greater volume, but lacks of course, in height. As already noted, the pyramids of the New World are simply foundations for temples and thus always have flat tops. The great mound of

Fig. 58. Pottery Plates from Cholula with Decorations in Several Colors. The pottery of Cholula ranks high in design and color.

Cholula is a solid mass of adobe bricks of uniform size laid in adobe mortar. The pyramid was evidently faced with a thick layer of cement of which a few patches still remain. Two other large mounds exist at Cholula. One of these has been partially destroyed and now stands as a vertical mass of adobe bricks while the other is overgrown with brush and cactus.

[a]

[b]

Plate XXXIV. (a) Partial View of the Great Pyramid at
Cholula which rises from the Level Plain in Three Broad Terraces.
A Spanish church has been built upon the top of this pyramid and
a roadway leads up the badly eroded mound. (b) A View at La
Quemada. Cylindrical columns built up of slabs of stone supported the roofs of some of the structures. The use of columns
was characteristic of late Toltecan times.

181

Unlike the other Toltecan cities Cholula was still inhabited and a place of religious importance when Cortez arrived in Mexico. But the figurines and pottery vessels that are found at this site belong for the most part to an epoch earlier than that of the Aztecs. Quetzalcoatl was the patron deity of Cholula and in the decorative art the serpent is finely conventionalized. A pottery shape frequently met with at Cholula is the flat plate bearing polychrome designs.

The Frontier Cities of the Northwest. An important culture area is located upon the northwestern limits of the area of high culture in ancient Mexico. The best known and most accessible ruin is La Quemada, "The Burned" which is situated a day's ride from the city of Zacatecas. This site was found in a deserted and ruinous condition by the Spaniards in 1535 and there is little doubt that it had been abandoned several centuries previous. La Quemada has been popularly associated with Chicomoztoc, "The Seven Caves," a place famous in Aztecan mythology, but this association rests upon no scientific basis. It is simply an unauthoritative attempt to invest a forgotten city with a legendary interest. Chicomoztoc, where the Aztecs came out of the underworld might be compared with our own Garden of Eden and its exact location is just as much an eternal riddle. La Quemada is a terraced hill resembling Monte Alban and Xochicalco. The retaining walls of terraces and pyramids as well as the walls of buildings are still well preserved. These walls consist of slabs of stone set in a mortar of red earth. Perhaps the most noteworthy structure is a wide hall containing seven columns built of slabs of stone in the same manner as the walls. All in all the architectural types as well as the observed contacts in art point to a late epoch of the Toltecan period. Other ruins of the same character as La Quemada occur at Chalchihuites on the frontier of Durango and at Totoate, etc., in northern Jalisco.

The most important artistic product from this northwestern region is a peculiar kind of pottery which might be described as cloisonné or encaustic ware. Examination shows that this pottery was first burned in the usual way so that it acquired a red or orange color. Then the surface was covered with a layer of greenish or blackish pigment to the depth of perhaps a sixteenth of an inch. A large part of this surface layer was then carefully cut away with a sharp blade in such a way that the remaining portions outlined certain geometric and realistic figures. The sunken spaces, from which the material had just been removed, were then filled in flush with red, yellow, white, and green pigments. The designs on this class of pottery are thus mosaics in which the different colors are separated by narrow lines of a neutral tint. The geometric motives show a marked use of the terrace, the fret, and the scroll. The realistic subjects are presented in a highly conventionalized manner and have few stylistic similarities to the figures from the Valley of Mexico. Representative collections of this ware from Totoate, already referred to, and from Estanzuela, a hacienda near Guadalajara, are on exhibition in the American Museum of Natural History.

Cloisonné pottery of a somewhat different style sometimes occurs at Toltecan sites in the Valley of Mexico, such as Tula, Teotihuacan, and Atzcapotzalco, but fresco pottery which resembles it at first glance is more characteristic. It appears that the cloisonné process was taken over from the embellishment of gourd dishes in connection with which it still exists over a large part of Mexico and Central America.

Another common method of ceramic decoration taken over was that of negative painting similar to the process used with cloth in making batik designs.

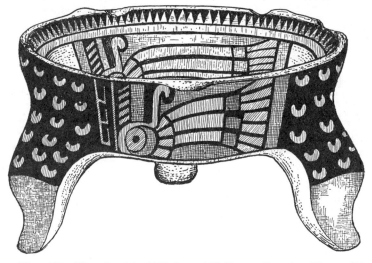

Fig. 59. Vessel with "Cloisonné" Decoration in Heavy Pigments. This example comes from a mound at Atzcapotzalco and dates from late Toltecan times. Trade pieces of this ware have been found at Pueblo Bonito in New Mexico and Chichen Itza in Yucatan.

This process still exists in Central America as regards gourd dishes although discontinued on pottery. Negative painting appears to be an ancient process of exceedingly wide distribution. It is especially common in Jalisco and Michoacan, the Valley of Toluca, Nicaragua, Costa Rica, Panama,

and Colombia, and sometimes occurs in Yucatan and
Peru. The design was painted in wax or some
other soluble or combustible paint, then the entire
surface was covered with a permanent paint.

Fig. 60. The Turtle Motive as developed in Negative Painting
with Wax at Totoate, Jalisco.

When the pot was burned the design came out in
the natural color of the clay against a black, or
sometimes a red field. The design was often made
two layers deep by applying simple masses of red
over the sizing before the impermanent paint of the
design proper was put on. In the northwestern
region of central Mexico now under consideration

Plate XXXV. Stone Slab from an Ancient
Sepulcher in the State of Guerrero. The face at
the top apparently represents a monkey, but
serpents have been introduced between the eyes
and the eyebrows. The other highly conventionalized faces are probably those of serpents.

186

the negative painting technique is associated with conventionalized designs representing turtles (Fig. 60). Another ware with designs in white is concerned with derivatives of the turtle motive. Then there are the remarkable copper bells in the form of turtles made by coiling, that have been found in nearby Michoacan.

Fig. 61. Jaguar Head on Disk-Shaped Stone. Salvador.

It is difficult to place time limits for the artistic styles that once existed in this northwestern region. The archaic culture seems to have lasted longer here than farther south; next followed the northern flow of Toltecan culture which later receded and finally came a rather thin layer of Chichimecan or Aztecan culture. We may tentatively conclude that the forgotten cities of the Zacatecan subculture flourished after 1000 A. D. The question should be settled because of its connection with the dating of Pueblo ruins farther north.

Santa Lucia Cozumalhualpa. The zonal distribution of rain forests in southern Mexico and Central America is especially important, as has been pointed out, in connection with the spread of Mayan-type civilizations. The Olmeca and Totonacs who were among the first to feel the cultural effects of the

Mayan ascendency occupied lands of heavy precipitation. The Zapotecan and Mixtecan areas were partly wet and partly dry. The Toltecs seem originally to have been desert dwellers but they extended their conquests over tribes living in the humid tropics and made much of cacao, rubber, copal, etc., obtained by trade and tribute from such subject peoples.

Along the Pacific coast below the Isthmus of Tehuantepec lies a rain belt containing ruined cities which flourished between 1000 to 1300 A. D., or on the historical level of the Toltec expansion. The sculptural art at these sites resembles the works attributed to the Olmecs in Tabasco and Vera Cruz on the one hand and to the works of the Chorotega of lower Central America on the other. One such ruin is Quiengola near the modern city of Tehuantepec, another occupies a ridge above Tonalá and there is a cluster of sites in the environs of Santa Lucia Cozumalhualpa in southern Guatemala, extending into western Salvador.

Whether or not the sculptures of Santa Lucia Cozumalhualpa are to be credited to the Pipil, a Mexican tribe, is far from certain, but human sacrifice and other Toltec religious ideas are plainly presented. We find here elaborate speech scrolls comparable to those of Xochicalco and the Toltec work at Chichen Itza. Also there is evidence of the ceremonial importance of cacao in this region, the god of this economic plant being pictured in the form of a jaguar.

A peculiar type of pottery centered in southern Guatemala and western Salvador from which region it was distributed far and wide by trade. Although a few examples of this ware are found at Copan it is clear from the designs that most of the pieces belong to a time subsequent to the abandonment of this Mayan city. The ware has a semi-glaze which is the result of lead in the clay. Because paint could not be applied to this ware, the esthetic idea of shape was allowed to develop itself without hindrance. This pottery is now referred to as plumbate ware.

The Chorotegan Culture. Passing south and east from the Mayan area we find remains of a rich and in many ways peculiar art, consisting mostly of pottery and stone carvings, to which the name Chorotegan is applied. This name means Driven-out People. It was first used in connection with several tribes of the Chiapanec-Otomi stock dispossessed of a fertile area about Lake Nicaragua by the intrusive Mexican-speaking Nicarao. The Chorotega were not, however, totally dispossessed since they continued to hold the Peninsula of Nicoya in Costa Rica as well as other pieces of territory. In an archæological sense the name Chorotegan fittingly can be extended to eastern parts of Costa Rica, Nicaragua, and Honduras, since the inhabitants of this stretch of land were also dispossessed some time before the coming of the Spaniards. Or perhaps they voluntarily migrated northward towards the end of the Toltec rule and are to be identified with the Otomi, Tlappaneca, and Mazateca of southern and central Mexico. The Tlappaneca and Otomi are definitely associated with introduction into Mexico of the peculiar cult of Xipe, God of the Flayed. This cult was clearly of southern origin and indeed still survived at Nicaragua at the time of the Spanish Conquest. The Mazateca were

found in transit by Cortez, in the southern part of
the Peninsula of Yucatan, living in palisaded villages. Similar palisaded villages once flourished
in Honduras. The wild South American tribes who
replaced the eastern Chorotega exhibit a cultural
non-conformity with the archæological remains of
the region they now occupy.

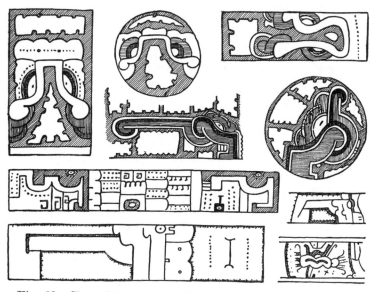

Fig. 62. Front View and Profile View Serpent Heads in Chorotegan Art. Although derived from Mayan models they have under-
gone great changes and have become highly conventionalized.

Close analysis shows that many of the decorative
motives in Chorotegan art were developed from
those of the Mayas. The serpent and the monkey
furnish the majority of the designs that are surely
Mayan but each of these is carried so far away from
the original that only an expert can see the connections. The arms and legs of the monkeys are
lengthened and given an extra number of joints

while the heads degenerate into circles. The tongues of the serpents are elongated and bent downward at the end. All the open spaces are treated with scallops or fringes of short lines.

Fig. 63. Jaguar Design with Mayan Affinities associated with Figurines that still retain Archaic Characters. Costa Rica.

Fig. 64. Jaguars from painted Nicoyan Vases.

There is also in Chorotegan art a crocodilian motive that may be peculiar to the Isthmian region although it has Mayan affinities. The jaguar is also important in this ancient art. Among the most interesting vases are those that have a modeled head projecting from one side (jaguar, monkey, or bird) and two of the three legs of the vessel modified

[a]   [b]   [c]

Plate XXXVI. (*a*) Finely Carved Ceremonial Slab found at Mercedes, Costa Rica. The three large figures on the end as well as the smaller ones on the bottom represent crocodiles. Keith Collection; (*b*) Stone Figure from Costa Rica. This sculpture in lava rock is one of the finest pieces ever discovered in this region. The lines on the body probably represent tattoo marks; (*c*) Ceremonial Slab decorated with Monkeys. Mercedes, Costa Rica. These ceremonial slabs may be developments of metates or corn grinders. Keith Collection.

192

into animal legs.   On these elaborate vessels there
are bands of painted decoration mostly concerned
with the crocodile.

The extremely elaborate metates (stones upon
which maize was ground) from southern Nicaragua
and northern Costa Rica probably were made by the
producers of the peculiar pottery art already described.   These were carved out of solid blocks of
lava with stone tools.   It is not unlikely that these
elaborate metates were used as ceremonial seats

Fig. 65.   Highly Conventionalized Jaguar Motive.   The principal
features of the head as well as the outline of the leg survive in highly
modified form.   From the southern end of Lake Nicaragua.

since few of them show signs of use.   The jaguar
is perhaps the most common motive used in the
decoration of these metates.   The back is broad
and slightly dished, the head projects from the center of one end and the tail swings in a curve from
the other end to one of the feet.

At Mercedes remarkable stone slabs were found
during the excavations conducted by Mr. Minor C.
Keith.   These are now on exhibition in the American Museum of Natural History.   The sculptures
in relief on these slabs are by all odds the finest
from the Isthmian area.   Human beings, crocodiles,

monkeys and birds are all used to decorate these carefully and laboriously made pieces whose use is entirely unknown. Statues in the full round have also been unearthed in quantity at Mercedes which

Fig. 66. Simple Crocodile Figures in Red Lines on Dishes from Mercedes, Costa Rica.

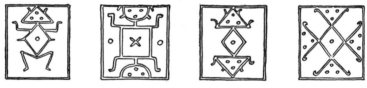

Fig. 67. Panels containing Crocodiles painted in White Lines on Large Tripod Bowls from Mercedes, Costa Rica.

Fig. 68. Simplified Crocodile Heads in the Yellow Line Ware of Mercedes, Costa Rica.

gives every evidence of having been a large city with a long career.

We may be reasonably sure that the stone slabs date from a fairly late epoch because an undoubted "Chacmool" exhibiting the same style of carving has been discovered here. The "Chacmool," a half reclining figure with the knees drawn up, the body supported in part upon the elbows and a bowl for incense or other offerings in the pit of the stomach, gets its fanciful name from Le Plongeon who discovered the original at Chichen Itza. But the unmistakable sculptures of this type were apparently developed by the highland tribes and the cult was introduced into northern Yucatan during the period of Mexican influence. In addition to Chichen Itza examples have been found at Cempoalan, the historic Totonacan capital near Vera Cruz, at Texcoco, in the Valley of Mexico, at Jhuatzio in the Tarascan region, as well as at Chalchuapa far to the southeast in Salvador. All of these occurrences indicate a late Toltecan horizon for its distribution.

Isthmian Gold Work. Metal-working was unknown to the Mayas of the First Empire, but is abundantly illustrated in cities of the Second Empire, especially Chichen Itza where the pieces are predominantly of Costa Rican and Colombian manufacture evidently secured in trade. We are therefore justified in concluding that the splendid Isthmian gold work came into being after 630 A. D. and was typically developed by 1200 A. D. The "wire technique," essentially a cast rather than a soldered filigree, characterized metal working as far south as southern Colombia and is also the dominant mode in Mexico. In addition to plain and hollow casting, two kinds of gold plating were carried to perfection by the ancient metal workers: one a heavy plating over copper and the other a thin gilding. The manner in which this plating was done is still uncertain. It has been suggested that the molds were lined with

Plate XXXVII. (*a*) The Gold Work of the Ancient Mexicans excited the Wonder of the Spanish Conquerors. Comparatively few examples, however, have come down to us; (*b*) Many Ornaments of Gold are found in the Graves of Costa Rica and Panama. The Keith Collection contains a very fine series of these pieces illustrating all the forms as well as the technical processes.

leaf gold or sprinkled with gold dust before the
baser copper was poured in.   Also acids are said
to have been used to dissolve out copper from the
surfaces.   Many ornaments are of pure beaten gold
and have designs in *repoussé*.

Fig. 69.   Conventional Crocodiles from Costa Rica and Panama.

The gold objects are found in stone box graves
along with pottery and stone carvings. Gold is
taken from only a small percentage of the graves,
probably those of chiefs. A systematic rifling of
the ancient cemeteries has been going on since the
arrival of the Spaniards, but the finds have mostly
been thrown into the melting pot. The burial
places are sometimes marked by low platforms built
over a group of graves. An iron rod, giving forth
a hollow sound when the stone cysts are struck, is
used by the searchers. Human bones are found in

these graves, but seldom in a state of good preservation.

Mr. Minor C. Keith's collection of gold work from Costa Rica and Panama is unexcelled and illustrates the range of technical processes as well as of ornamental forms. Human forms are represented with peculiar headdresses and with various objects carried in the hands and often they are joined in pairs. Many of the most beautiful amulets are frogs arranged either singly or in groups of two or three. These figures are all provided with a ring on the under side for suspension. Lizards, turtles, and crocodiles are frequently modeled as well as clam shells, crabs, and monkeys. But perhaps the most frequent amulets are those that picture birds with outspread wings among which may be recognized vultures, harpy eagles, gulls, man-of-war birds, and parrots. The larger and more elaborate pieces of gold work cast considerable light on the ancient religion of the natives since beast gods are figured in half human form. Bells of copper and gold were much used in gala dress and were doubtless an object of trade with the tribes farther north.

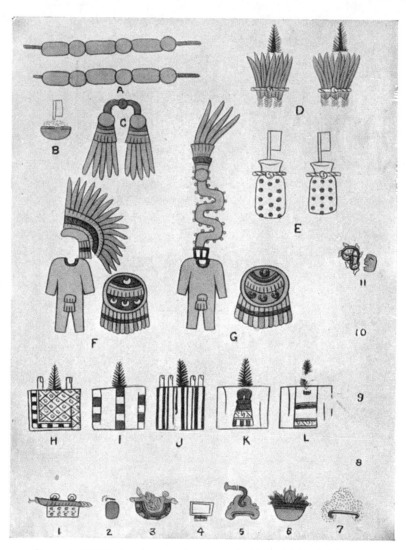

Plate XXXVIII. A Page from the Tribute Roll of Moctezuma, showing the Annual Tribute of the Eleven Towns pictured at the Bottom and Right. The tribute consisted of: (*a*) Two strings of jade beads; (*b*) Twenty gourd dishes of gold dust; (*c*) A royal headdress; (*d*) Eight hundred bunches of feathers; (*e*) Forty bags of cochineal dye; (*f–g*) Warrior's costumes; (*h*) Four hundred and two blankets of this pattern; (*i*) Four hundred blankets; (*j*) Four hundred and four blankets; (*k*) Four hundred blankets. The towns are: (1) Coaxalahuacan; (2) Texopan; (3) Tamozolapan; (4) Yancuitlan; (5) Tezuzcululan; (6) Nochistlan; (7) Xaltepec; (8) Tamazolan; (9) Mictlan (Mitla); (10) Coaxomulcu; (11) Cuicatlan, in the State of Oaxaca.

CHAPTER IV

THE AZTECS

THE Aztecs were the dominant nation on the highlands of Mexico when Cortez marched with his small army to conquer New Spain. The horrible sacrifices that they made to their gods and the wealth and barbaric splendor of their rulers have often been described. But their history in point of time covered short space and their art and religion was based in a large measure on achievements of the nations that had preceded them.

Mayas and Aztecs compared to Greeks and Romans. A remarkably close analogy may be drawn between the Mayas and Aztecs in the New World and the Greeks and Romans in the Old, as regards character, achievements, and relations one to the other. The Mayas, like the Greeks, were an artistic and intellectual people who developed sculpture, painting, architecture, astronomy, and other arts and sciences to a high plane. Politically, both were divided into communities or states that bickered and quarreled. There were temporary leagues between certain cities, but real unity only against a common enemy. Culturally, both were one people, in spite of dialectic differences, for the warring factions were bound together by a common religion and a common thought. To be sure the religion of the Mayas was much more barbaric than that of the Greeks but in each case the subject matter was idealized and beautified in art.

The Aztecs, like the Romans, were a brusque and

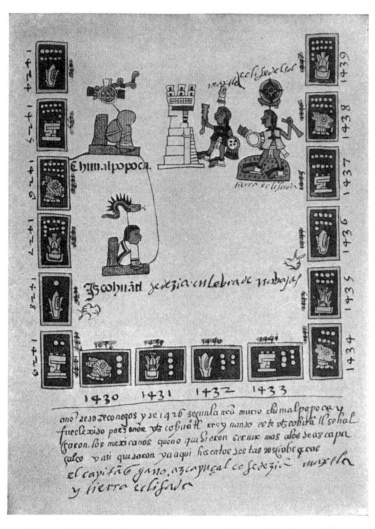

Plate XXXIX. Page from the Codex Telleriano-Remensis showing a Native Manuscript with Explication by the Spaniards. The death of Chimalpopoca and the election of his successor, Itzcouatl, is recorded, as well as the capture of Atzcapotzalco.

202

warlike people who built upon the ruins of an earlier civilization that fell before the force of their arms and who made their most notable contributions to organization and government. The Toltecs stand just beyond the foreline of Aztecan history and may fitly be compared to the Etruscans. They were the possessors of a culture derived in part from their brilliant contemporaries that was magnified to true greatness by their ruder successors.

The Chichimecas. The term Chichimecas was applied by the more civilized tribes of the Mexican highlands to those nomads outside the pale who dressed in skins and hunted with the bow and arrow. Some of these wandering groups spoke Nahuan dialects, but the term was also applied to the Otomis who spoke a distinct language. Possibly through having been reduced in war certain of these wandering groups were drawn into civilization and when the Toltecan cities began to decline, they advanced to considerable power and prestige. In fact, the Aztecs may be considered as originally Chichimecan, along with the people of Texcoco. In later times, these city-broken nomads looked back with considerable pride on their lowly origin. The early life in the open is pictured interestingly in several documents including the Map of Tlotzin and the Map of Quinatzin.

We have already seen how the splendid culture of the Toltecan cities broke down under the weight of civil war about 1220 A. D. To be sure, Cholula appears to have kept alive the flame of Toltecan religion and art up to the advent of the Spaniards. Atzcapotzalco, Colhuacan, and other towns near the lakes that had been established during the Toltecan period were able to hold their own for a time against the newer order.

Xolotl, founder of the dynasty of Texcoco, makes his first appearance in the Valley of Mexico in 1225, five years after the dispersion of the Toltecs, according to the Codex Xolotl. He viewed the abandoned cities but neither he nor his immediate successors chose to lead a sedentary life. The first date appears too early because it seems unlikely that the reigns of Xolotl and his son actually covered ninety years. The foundation of Texcoco took place in the reign of Techotlala and Ixtlilxochitl, his son, fell a victim to the murderous policy of Tezozomoc, the famous tyrant of Atzcapotzalco. Nezahualcoyotl, who regained the throne in 1431 was a great poet, philosopher, and law maker. The rulers of Texcoco were as follows:—

THE DYNASTY OF TEXCOCO

NOMADIC CHIEFTAINS

Xolotl	1225–1284
Nopalli	1284–1315
Tlotzin	1315–1324
Quinatzin	1324–1357

SEDENTARY CHIEFTAINS

Techotlala	1357–1409
Ixtlilxochitl	1409–1418
(Interregnum)	1418–1431
Nezahualcoyotl	1431–1472
Nezahualpilli	1472–1515
Cacama	1515–1520

Aztecan History. The history of the Aztecs has a mythological preamble in common with other nations of Mexico. The Chicomoztoc or Seven Caves must not be considered historical but simply man's place of emergence from the underworld. The general conception of an existence within the earth that preceded the existence upon the earth is found very widely among North American Indians. It is likewise impossible to locate the Island of Aztlan, that served, according to several codices, as the starting place of the Mexican migration. The northern origin for the Aztecan tribe to which so much attention has been paid need not have been far from the Valley of Mexico, since in their entire recorded peregrination they hardly traveled eighty miles.

Owing to the ineffectiveness of the Mexican time count Aztecan chronology is far from fixed. The year was known by the day with which it began and as this day ran the permutation of four names and thirteen numbers a cycle was fifty-two years in length. No method of keeping the cycles in their proper order seems to have been devised except the laborious one of putting down every year in sequence whether or not an event occurred in it. According to different authorities the year 1 Stone which begins the historical account in the Aubin Codex was 648, 1064, or 1168 in the European calendar, each date differing from the others by multiples of fifty-two years. The last base, 1168, is correct; this being the epoch of the Toltec Era established by Quetzalcoatl.

The wandering tribes, among which may be mentioned the Chalca, Xochimilca, Tlahuica, Huexotzinca, Tepaneca, and Azteca, pushed their way into the region of the lakes and were allowed to live in less desirable locations as vassals to the established tribes. The "peregrinations" relate the succession of stops and the length of each stop. The Aztecs themselves made twenty or more stops lasting from

Plate XL. Serpent Head at Bottom of Balustrade, Great Pyramid, Mexico City. The same excavations showed that the Great Pyramid was enlarged several times and this sculpture seems to have been buried under the walls long before the coming of the Spaniards. Compare Serpent Balustrade at Chichen Itza.

206

two to twenty years. Finally, about 1325, they reached Chapultepec and for a number of years lived in comparative peace and quiet. Their bad manners and growing power excited the enmity of several nearby towns and in 1351 the Aztecs, under their chieftain Huitzili- huitl, were worsted in a fierce battle. Remnants of the tribe, including Huitzilihuitl and his daughter, sought the protection of Cozcoztli, king of Colhuacan. They soon were able to repay his support in a war with Xochimilco. The first actual settle- ment on the site of the future Tenoch- titlan was made in 1364 and in 1376 Acamapictli, a noble allied to the royal house of Colhuacan, was elected to be the first war chief of the new city.

Fig. 70. Pic- tographic Rec- ord of fighting near the Springs of Chapultepec, "Hill of the Grasshopper." Aubin Codex.

One of the first improvements un- dertaken by the new city was in the matter of water supply. Rights were secured to the famous spring of Cha- pultepec, an important gain because the brackish waters of the lake were not fit to drink. A double water main of terra cotta was laid from the springs to the town. New land was made, prob- ably after the manner still to be seen in the famous floating gardens of Xochimilco by throwing the soil from the bed of the shallow lake into enclosed areas of wattle work. Gradually a Venice-like city, trav- ersed by canals and admirably protected from at- tack, rose from the lake. At the coming of the Spaniards there were three causeways leading to the shores of the lake and each of these was pro-

tected by drawbridges. There was a city wall upon
which were lighthouses for the guidance of home-
coming fishermen. There were palaces and market
places and a great central plaza called the Tecpan,
where were situated the principal temples.

The Spaniards destroyed the ancient city, block-
ing up the canals with the débris of temples, and
building the new City of Mexico over the leveled
ruins. Ancient relics are brought to light wherever
excavations are made. In 1900 many sculptures
and ceremonial objects were uncovered in Escaleri-
llas street near the Cathedral. Recently a building
near the National Museum was torn down for re-
placement and in digging for new foundations part
of the base of the great pyramid was found. This
had been enlarged several times, as could be seen
by the stairways successively buried under new
walls. At the bottom of the balustrade of one stairway a great serpent head of stone was found in its
original position (Plate XL).

The Aztecs count their history as a great people
from their first war chief Acamapichtli who com-
menced his rule in 1376 (Codex Aubin). The names
and the order of the succeeding war chiefs are the
same in several records, but the dates are found to
vary slightly.

Acamapichtli	1376–1396
Huitzilihuitl	1396–1417
Chimalpopoca	1417–1427
Itzcouatl	1427–1440
Moctezuma I	1440–1469
Axayacatl	1469–1482
Tizoc	1482–1486
Ahuitzotl	1486–1502
Moctezuma II	1502–1520
Cuitlahua	1520
Cuauhtemoc	1520–1521

After throwing off the yoke of their early over-
lords, the Tepanecas, by the subjection of Atzcapotzalco at the beginning of the brilliant reign of
Itzcouatl, the Aztecs of Tenochtitlan entered into a
three-cornered league with Texcoco and Tlacopan
(Tacuba). This was an offensive and defensive alliance with an equal division of the spoils of war.
Soon the united power of these three cities dom-
inated the Valley of Mexico and began to be felt
across the mountains on every side. Tenochtitlan
gradually assumed the commanding position in the
league, and although Texcoco continued to be an
important center the third member was apparently
much reduced. The great votive stone of Tizoc records some of the earlier conquests of the Aztecs.
At the arrival of Cortez only a few important cities
such as Tlaxcala retained their independence. But
the crest of power had then been passed and it
seems pretty certain that the remarkable city in the
lake would in time have suffered the fate of other
self-constituted capitals both in the Old World and
the New.

Social Organization. Spanish historians often
liken Tenochtitlan to the seat of an empire and
speak of the ruler as one who had the power of an
absolute monarch while other and more recent writers have declared that the tribal organization of the
Aztecs was essentially democratic. The truth
doubtless lies between these extremes. The people
were warlike by nature and all men, except a few
of the priesthood, were soldiers. Honors depended
largely upon success in war and warriors were arranged in ranks according to their deeds. The
common warriors formed one rank and next came

those who had distinguished themselves by definite achievements which gave the right to wear certain articles of dress or to bear certain titles. The chiefs were elected for an indefinite term of office from the most distinguished fighters and could be removed for cause.

But while the offices of state were elective there was, nevertheless, a tendency to choose from certain powerful families and at least the foundation of an aristocratic policy. A chief was succeeded by his son or brother except when these candidates were manifestly unfit. In the actual succession of the great war chiefs of Tenochtitlan, a peculiar system seems to have been followed in that the candidates from the older generation were ordinarily exhausted before the next lower generation became eligible. Thus Huitzilihuitl, Chimalpopoca, and Itzcouatl were all sons of Acamapichtli, and the last and greatest was born of a slave mother. Then followed Moctezuma Ilhuicamina I, the son of Huitzilihuitl. This chief had no male heirs but the children of his daughter ruled in order: Axayacatl, Tizoc, and Ahuitzotl. Moctezuma II was the son of the first of these as was Cuitlahua, while Cuauhtemoc, the last Aztec ruler, was the son of Ahuitzotl. This peculiar succession was not in vogue in Texcoco, where son succeeded father and the lawful wife was chosen from the royalty of Tenochtitlan. In the various annals, the genealogies are often indicated and the evidence that aristocracies existed is too strong to be overthrown. There are even cases of queens who succeeded to the chief power after the death of the royal husband.

It is extremely doubtful whether the Aztecs ever had what might be called clans. We have seen that there were originally eight closely related tribes constituting the Mexica or Mexici nation. The Aztecs themselves are said to have been divided into seven groups that were first reduced to four or five and then increased to about twenty. It is not clear that these were exogamic kinship groups. They were probably military societies taking into their membership all the men of the tribe. The name *Calpolli,* or "great house," which was applied to them seems to have referred to a sort of barracks or general meeting place in each ward or division of the city where arms and trophies were kept and the youth educated in the art of war. The title in land was held by the *calpolli* and the right of use distributed among the heads of families who held possession only so long as the land was worked. Each *calpolli* seems to have had a certain autonomy in governmental matters as well as a local religious organization. It is curious to find in Salvador, far to the south, the word *calpolli* applied to the platform mounds that surround courts in the ancient ruins. This use of the word may indicate that the "great houses" of the different societies were ordinarily the principal buildings of the city and that they were used for civil, military, and religious purposes.

In forming judgment on the fundamentals of social organization among the Aztecs we must remember that no clear case of kinship clans has been reported south of the area of the United States. Among the Cakchiquels, a Mayan tribe of the Guatemalan highlands, two royal houses are reported from which the ruling chief was alternately drawn. The Zotzils have been explained as a bat clan because their name is associated with the word for

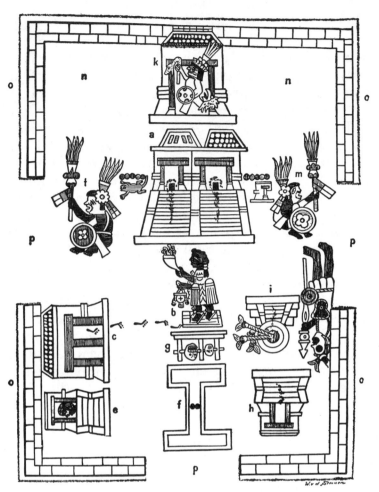

Plate XLI.   Sahagun's Plan of the Tecpan in Mexico City.   After
Seler.   Among the details shown are: (*a*) The two great temples;
(*b*) The *Quauhxicalli* or eagle bowl; (*c*) One of the *Callimecatl*, or
priest houses; (*e*) An eagle house or warriors' shrine; (*f*) The *Te-
otlachtli* or ball court of the gods; (*g*) *Tzompantli* or skull rack;
(*h*) The temple of Xipi; (*i*) The *Temalacatl* or Gladiator Stone;
(*k*) The *Colhuacan Teocalli* or temple of Colhuacan; (*l–m*) The
gods 5 Lizard and 5 House respectively; (*n*) Dance courts; (*o*)
Coatenamitl or Serpent Wall, so called because it was decorated
with heads of serpents.

bat and because a bat god appears to have been their patron deity. The Mazatecas and Mixtecas, Deer people and Cloud people, also have clanlike names but in all cases these are designations of entire tribes, not of subdivisions of tribes.

Tenochtitlan was divided into four quarters and each quarter subdivided into a number of wards. An under chief was elected from each of the subdivisions which are doubtless to be identified with the *calpolli,* and an over chief from each of the four quarters. Above these stood the war chief of the entire tribe who was likewise elected, but within the limits of a fixed aristocracy. A second great chief, who seems to have been a peace officer with some important relation to the priesthood, was nominally equal to the war chief, but practically much less powerful. The real center of the home government was a council made up of all the chiefs. In time of war the war chief was in supreme command and could either delegate his rights or act in person. Just how much the priesthood intervened in governmental affairs cannot be definitely put in words, but their power was doubtless great. Certain lands were cultivated in common for the officers of church and state and much of the tribute from conquered provinces was devoted to their needs.

The Tecpan or Temple Enclosure. The ceremonial center of Tenochtitlan has been transformed into the civic center of Mexico City. The Cathedral, the National Palace, and the Zocolo, or Plaza Major, mark the site where once stood the famous Tecpan or temple enclosure. Within the serpent walls, according to Sahagun, there were twenty-five temple pyramids, five oratories, sundry fasting

Plate XLII. The Calendar Stone of the Aztecs. This great stone represents the disk of the sun and the history of the world. It may be analyzed as follows, reading outward from the center.

Central or cosmogonic portion: The day sign 4 Olin with details in the arms representing four epochs of the world; with the face of the sun god in the center and minor hieroglyphs that may represent the four directions just outside the Olin symbol.

Band of day signs beginning at the top and reading towards the left.

Bands of conventional rays of the sun and other details such as the embellishment of the sun with turquoise and eagle feathers.

The outer circle of two great reptiles that may indicate the universe.

Invisible edge of the disk bears representations of Itzpapalotl, the obsidian butterfly which is symbolical of the heavens.

214

houses, four bowl-shaped stones, one disk-shaped stone, a great stepped altar, a "star column," seven skull racks, two ball courts, two enclosed areas, a well, three bathing places, two cellar-like rooms, a dancing place, nine priest houses, a prison for the gods of conquered nations, arsenals, work places, etc. A native plan of the Tecpan, much simplified, occurs in the Sahagun manuscript. The great pyramid rose in several terraces and was surmounted by two temples each three stories in height, one dedicated to Huitzilopochtli and the other to Tlaloc. Each temple contained an image of the god to which it was dedicated and a sacrificial altar. The walls were encrusted with blood of human victims whose hearts, still beating, had been torn out for divine food and whose bodies had been rolled down the steep flight of temple stairs. The foundations for the great pyramids were laid in 1447 by Moctezuma I, the pyramids were completed in 1485 while Tizoc was war chief and the final dedication ceremonies were held in 1487.

Several very interesting large sculptures and many minor objects have been unearthed on the site of the Tecpan. In 1790 and 1791 were found three famous monoliths, the Calendar Stone, the Stone of Tizoc (Sacrificial Stone), and the Statue of Coatlicue. Since 1897 many fine pieces of pottery and several sculptures have been excavated near the Cathedral and placed in the Museo Nacional.

The Calendar Stone. The great sculptured monument known as the Calendar Stone or Stone of the Sun, is the most valuable object that has come down intact from the time of the Aztecs. It is a single piece of porphyry, irregular except for the sculp-

Plate XLIII. The Shield Stone at Cuernavaca. This Aztecan sculpture carved upon a boulder in the City of Cuernavaca shows a shield, a bundle of war arrows, and a war banner. The sculpture records the conquest of Cuernavaca or more properly Quauhnahuac, capital of the Tlahuican nation.

216

tured face. It now weighs over twenty tons and it
is estimated that the original weight was over twice
as much. The sculptured disk is about twelve feet
in diameter. This great stone was transported by
men over many miles of marshy lake bottom before
it could be placed in position in front of the Temple
of the Sun in the temple enclosure that has just
been described. The stone was doubtless thrown
down from its original position by the soldiers of
Cortez and may have been lost to sight. We know,
however, that it was exposed to view about 1560 and
was then buried by order of the archbishop of Mexico City lest its presence should cause the Indians
to revert to their original pagan beliefs. It was re-
discovered in 1790 and was afterwards built into the
façade of the Cathedral where it remained until
1885, when it was removed to the nearby museum.

The Calendar Stone is not only a symbol of the
sun's face marked with the divisions of the year
but it is a record of the cosmogonic myth of the
Aztecs and the creations and destructions of the
world. In the center is the face of the sun god,
Tonatiuh, enclosed in the middle of the symbol
called Olin. Tonatiuh is often represented by a
much simpler sign of a circle with four or more
subdivisions resembling those of a compass which
are intended to represent the rays of the sun. Olin
is one of the day signs and means movement, or perhaps earthquake. It has also been explained as a
graphic representation of the apparent course of
the sun during the year. The history of the world,
according to the Aztecan myth, is divided into five
suns or ages, four of which refer to the past and
one to the present. The present sun is called Olin
Tonatiuh because it is destined to be destroyed by

an earthquake. The day signs of the four previous suns are represented in the rectangular projections of the central Olin symbol beginning at the upper right hand corner and proceeding to the left. They are 4 Ocelotl (jaguar) ; 4 Ehecatl (wind) ; 4 Quauhtli (rain) ; 4 Atl (water), and they refer to destruction, first, by jaguars, second, by a hurricane, third, by a volcanic rain of fire, fourth, by a flood. It is claimed by some that the year 13 Acatl (reed) recorded at the top of the monument between the reptile tails refers to the first year of the present sun. The fifth sun will end with the day 4 Olin, that is expressed in the central symbol already described. For this reason a fast was held on each recurrence of this day. Outside of the Olin symbol but between its arms are four hieroglyphs of uncertain meaning. Next to this area dealing with the great ages of the world comes a band of the twenty day signs of the Aztecan month. Outside of this band are several others which probably represent in a conventionalized manner the rays of the sun and the turquoise and eagle feathers with which the sun disk was believed to be decorated. Finally, outside of all, are two plumed monsters meeting face to face at the bottom of the disk. In each reptile face is seen a human face in profile. These reptiles are probably to be identified as the Xiuhcoatl or Fire Serpents.

The newly discovered National Stone pictures the Calendar Stone in vertical position on a mound and at the head of a flight of steps. The dates on the side of the stairway are 1 Tochtli and 2 Acatl, 1506 and 1507, indicating that the Calendar Stone was dedicated in connection with the New Fire Ceremony. The design on the back of this new-found monument pictures the eagle on the cactus, symbolic of the founding of Tenochtitlan. Other sculptures adorn the sides, the top, and the bottom of the stone.

Stone of Tizoc. The Sacrificial Stone or Stone of Tizoc is believed to have been carved by order of Tizoc, the war chief who ruled from 1482–1486, as a memorial offering to Mexican arms on the completion of the great temple to the Mexican God of War. The stone was a *quauhxicalli,* or "eagle bowl." This name was given to large bowls which were used to hold the blood and the heart of human victims sacrificed to the gods. The same name was extended to the large drum-shaped stone, under consideration, which has a pit in the center and a sort of canal running from the center to one side which

Fig. 71. Details from the Stone of Tizoc: *a,* Huitzilopochtli, Aztec War God; *b,* Figures representing a captured town; *c,* Name of the captured town (Tuxpan, place of the rabbit).

may have been intended to drain off the blood. Human sacrifice actually took place on this stone but it is pretty certain that it was not one of the *temala-catl* or "gladiator stones" on which were staged mortal combats as ceremonies. According to description the gladiator stones were pierced by a hole in the center so that one or more captives could be bound fast by a rope.

On the top of the Stone of Tizoc is a representa-

Plate XLIV. The newly discovered "National Stone" of Mexico. The front view shows the Calendar Stone in position and the year signs 1 Rabbit and 2 Reed (1506 and 1507 A. D.). The sculpture on the back is an eagle on a cactus, recording the foundation of Mexico City (Tenochtitlan). On all the other surfaces priests and religious symbols are drawn.

tion of Tonatiuh, or the sun's disk, much less complex than that which we have seen on the Calendar Stone but with many similar parts. On the sides of the stone are fifteen groups of figures, each group representing a conqueror and his captive. The victorious soldier appears each time in the guise of the war god, Huitzilopochtli, or his wizard brother Tezcatlipoca. The left foot of the figure ends in two scroll-like objects that may represent the humming bird feathers that formed the left foot of Huitzilopochtli. But Tezcatlipoca also had a deformed foot. Moreover, on the side of the headdress is a disk with a flame-shaped object coming out of it. This may represent the smoking mirror of Tezcatlipoca. The captive wears costumes that change slightly from one figure to the next. Over the head of the captive in each instance is the hieroglyph of a captured town or district.

Nearly all the place name hieroglyphs have been deciphered. The list is interesting historically because it gives the principal conquests up to the reign of Tizoc. Starting at the side directly across the stone from the groove or drain we see that the figure of the victor has behind his head a hieroglyph that represents a leg. This is the hieroglyph of Tizoc and the victim in this case represents the district of Matlatzinco in the Valley of Toluca. This district was brought under subjection by Tizoc himself. Among the other conquered cities are such well-known ones as Chalco, Xochimilco, and Colhuacan in the vicinity of Lake Texcoco and Ahuilizapan (Orizaba) and Tuxpan that are more distant.

Coatlicue. The famous statue of the Earth Goddess, Coatlicue, "the goddess with the serpent

Plate XLV. Monstrous Sculpture representing Coatlicue, the Serpent-Skirted Goddess, who was regarded as the Mother of the Gods.

skirt,'' is one of the most striking examples of
barbaric imagination. The name Teoyamiqui is
often given to this uncouth figure, but the identification is faulty. Like the other great sculptures we
have just examined, it doubtless occupied an important place in the great ceremonial center of
Tenochtitlan, but no ancient reference to it is extant.
This goddess is reported to have been the mother
of the gods.

Fig. 72. Detail showing the Construction of the Face of Coatlicue from Two Serpent Heads meeting End to End.

The statue may be described as follows: The feet
are furnished with claws. The skirt is a writhing
mass of braided rattlesnakes. The arms are dou-
bled up and the hands are snake heads on a level
with the shoulders. Around the neck and hanging
down over the breast is a necklace of alternating
hands and hearts with a death's head pendant. The
head of this monstrous woman is the same on front
and back and is formed of two serpent heads that
meet face to face. The forked tongue and the four
downward pointing fangs belong half and half to
each of the two profile faces.

Mexican Writing. The means of record employed in Mexican codices are in part pictographic
and in part hieroglyphic. The sequence of the historical events in these native manuscripts is often

indicated by a line of footprints leading from one place or scene of action to another. Historical records of this type resemble old-fashioned maps and some are actually called maps. The names of towns in these documents are represented by true hieroglyphs and often the character of the country is

Fig. 73. Hieroglyphs of Precious Materials: left to right, gold; turquoise; mosaic of precious stones; *chalchihuitl,* or jade; mirror of obsidian.

indicated by pictures of typical vegetation, such as maguey plants for the highlands and palms for the lowlands. The day or the year in which took place the foundation of the town or whatever event is intended to be recorded is usually placed in conjunction with the hieroglyph or picture. Conquest is indicated by a place name hieroglyph with a spear

tlan from *tlantli,* teeth

cal from *calli,* house

mix from *mixtla,* cloud

Fig. 74. Phonetic Elements derived from Pictures and used in Mexican Place Name Hieroglyphs.

thrust into it or by a temple on fire, while warfare is a shield and bundle of lances encircled by footprints.

A few examples of Nahuan hieroglyphs will now be given to illustrate this interesting method of writing. It must be remembered that there is nothing in the nature of a connected narrative.

The hieroglyphs or word pictures are limited to geographical and personal names, including the names of gods, to months, days, numbers, objects of commerce and a few objects or ideas of ceremonial import. Some of the signs are in no degree realistic and have a definite meaning by common consent alone, such as the symbol for gold (Fig. 73). Others are abbreviated and conventionalized pic-

Caltepec   Itztepec   Atepec   Pantepec

Miztlan   Itztlan   Petlatlan   Tecalco

Fig. 75. Aztecan Place Names.

tures of objects. Thus the head of a god or of an animal frequently appears as the sign of the whole. But the most important and interesting word signs are rebuses in which separate syllables or groups of syllables are represented by more or less conventionalized pictures. The whole word picture is a combination of syllable pictures which indicate phonetically the word as a whole. Very often advantage is taken of puns on whole or partial words, while color and position are also employed to indicate sounds and syllables.

In Fig. 74 are given a few of the more common
syllable pictures. The name of the object represented is cut down by the elimination of *tl, li,* etc.,

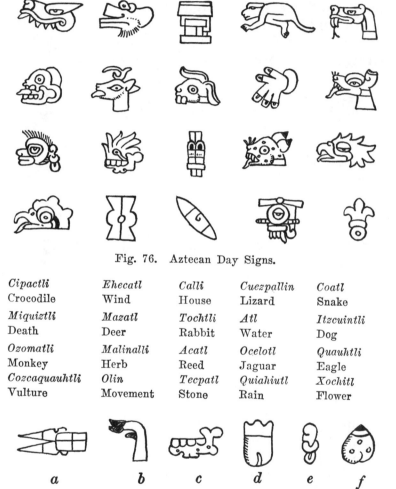

Fig. 76. Aztecan Day Signs.

Cipactli	*Ehecatl*	*Calli*	*Cuezpallin*	*Coatl*
Crocodile	Wind	House	Lizard	Snake
Miquiztli	*Mazatl*	*Tochtli*	*Atl*	*Itzcuintli*
Death	Deer	Rabbit	Water	Dog
Ozomatli	*Malinalli*	*Acatl*	*Ocelotl*	*Quauhtli*
Monkey	Herb	Reed	Jaguar	Eagle
Cozcaquauhtli	*Olin*	*Tecpatl*	*Quiahiutl*	*Xochitl*
Vulture	Movement	Stone	Rain	Flower

a	*b*	*c*	*d*	*e*	*f*

Fig. 77. Variant Forms of Aztecan Day Signs: *a, acatl,* arrow;
b, mazatl, deer foot; *c, malinalli,* jaw bone; *d, itzcuintli,* dog's ear;
e, ozomatli, monkey's ear; *f, ocelotl,* jaguar's ear.

that form the nominal endings. Thus, the picture of water, *atl*, becomes the sign for the sound *a*, that of stone *tetl* is cut down to the syllable *te*. Several of these syllable pictures are combined to represent a whole word.

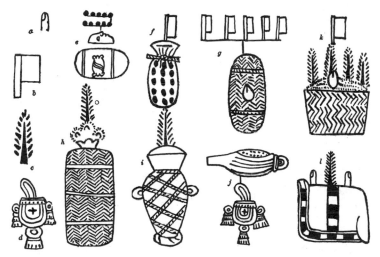

Fig. 78. Aztecan Numbers and Objects of Commerce: *a*, 1; *b*, 20; *c*, 400; *d*, 8,000; *e*, ten faces carved from precious stone; *f*, twenty bags of cochineal dye; *g*, one hundred bales of cocoa; *h*, four hundred bales of cotton; *i*, four hundred jars of honey of tuna; *j*, eight thousand leaf bundles of copal gum; *k*, twenty baskets each containing sixteen hundred ground cacao nibs; *l*, four hundred and two blankets.

The hieroglyphs of the twenty days of the month (see Fig. 76) are frequently represented, but those of the eighteen months are not nearly so well known. As for the gods, the faces are usually pictured, especially when these are grotesque, but sometimes details of dress or an object connected with a special ceremony is sufficient to recall the divinity. The Mexican system of numbers was based on twenties.

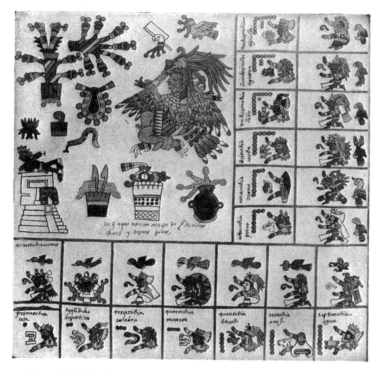

Plate XLVI. Page from the *Tonalamatl* Section of the Codex Borbonicus. The thirteen days run along the bottom of the page and up the right side of the large division. The period covered is one-twentieth of the *Tonalamatl* of 260 days. At the left of each day is seen one of the nine Lords of the Night, so-called, in orderly succession. In the divisions above or to the left of the days are the thirteen gods of the Hours of the Day in connection with the Thirteen Birds. The patron goddess of this division of the *Tonalamatl* is Itzpapalotl, the obsidian butterfly. The other pictures relate mostly to mythological instances and the details of ceremonies. For instance, the broken tree represents Tamoanchan, a legendary site, and the sacrifice of twenty birds is indicated by the flag attached to the bleeding head of a decapitated bird.

The units were figured by dots, the twenties by flags, the four hundreds by a device like a tree that represented hair, and the eight thousands by the ceremonial pouches in which copal incense was carried.

Aztecan Religion. The religion of the Aztecs, like that of the Mayas, was a polytheism in which special divinities controlled the powers of nature and the activities of men. The gods were perhaps further advanced towards human form and attributes than were those of the earlier culture to the south, but definite characterization was still accomplished by grotesque features and certain animal connections were still evident. The matter is confused beyond the point of analysis. The mythologies often ascribe different origins to the same deity. One god is addressed by many names, descriptive or figurative, that are intended to bring out the various aspects of his power. Overlapping functions make it impossible to assign each god to his special province. There are universal gods, there are special gods, and there are patron gods of trade guilds. Moreover, there are foreign gods, some recent, some ancient.

The religion of central Mexico had its objective, ritualistic side, which appealed directly to the understanding of the masses, and its more subtle theological or philosophical side seen, for instance, in the poems written by priests and rulers. It was a mixture of spirituality and the grossest idolatry. The ceremonial calendar, with a description of the feasts and sacrifices occurring at different times of the year, has been preserved in a number of documents. Pageants, incense-burning, and human sacrifice gave a strong dramatic quality to the religious rites.

[a]

[b]

Plate XLVII. (a) Pictures of Tlaloc, the God of Rain, and of Ehecatl, the God of Winds, in the Codex Magliabecchiano; (b) Mexican Genealogical Table on Bark Paper. The names of most of the individuals are given by hieroglyphs attached to the head or the seat. Original in the American Museum.

230

The conception of a supreme deity is seen in *Ome-teuctli,* the Lord of Duality, a vague god-head and creator who is sometimes addressed in some of the religious poems as the "Cause of All." In the background of the popular religion was the belief in the Earth Mother and the Sky Father and in the divinity of the Sun, the Moon, the Jaguar, the Serpent, and whatever else was beautiful, power-ful, a n d inexplicable. Tezcatlipoca, by reason of his magic and his omniscience, was placed at the head of the pan-theon of active gods. Huitzilopochtli was, how-ever, the favorite god of the Aztecs through his re-lation to war. Tlaloc, the god of rain, was naturally of great importance to agriculturists living in a rather arid region. To-natiuh, the Sun God, was a more or less abstract deity who acted in part through other gods. But the list is too long to be repeated here.

Fig. 79. Analysis of Mexi-can Record. 1, the year Two Reed, 1507; 2, eclipse of the sun; 3, earthquake at place pic-tured at 4; 5, the town of Huixachtitlan. In the temple (6) was held (7) the new-fire ceremony at the beginning of a 52-year period. In this year were also drowned in the River Tuzac (8) two thousand war-riors (10) which the vultures devoured (9).

The special gods of five principal Mexican cities were as follows:—

Tenochtitlan	Huitzilopochtli
Texcoco	Tezcatlipoca
Tlaxcala	Camaxtli
Cholula	Quetzalcoatl
Cuauhnahuac	Xochiquetzalli

Of gods with a foreign origin perhaps the most important were Quetzalcoatl and Xipe. The for-

Fig. 80. Chalchuihtlicue, Aztecan Goddess of Water.

mer was introduced long before the Aztecs raised their banner of war and was the Long-nosed God of the Mayas, introduced under the patronage of Quetzalcoatl, the powerful emperor of the Toltecs. The worship of Xipe is said to have originated in a town in southern Mexico. It had certainly taken a strong hold on the Aztecs of Mexico City and was likewise known as far south as Salvador. It has recently been demonstrated that the people of Yopico, specially given to the worship of Xipe, originated in Nicaragua.

Conceptions of the Universe. Cosmogonic myths, the world over, are unscientific attempts to explain the creation of the universe, to outline the powers of the gods and to trace the development of nature. The cosmogonic myths of Mexico and Central America are characterized by multiple creations. The Aztecan belief in five suns each standing for a world epoch is paralleled in fragments of Mayan mythology. Creation is not emphasized so much as destruction. The sequence of the suns is figured on the Calendar Stone, and in one of the codices, besides being explained in some of the early writings of Spanish priests and educated natives. The first sun was devoured by a jaguar and in the resulting darkness the inhabitants of the earth were devoured by jaguars. The second sun was destroyed by a hurricane, the third by a rain of fire, and the fourth by a flood. One human pair escaped each cataclysm and lived to repopulate the world. The fifth or present sun will be destroyed by an earthquake.

Notions of the shape and character of the universe are pretty well defined in Aztecan lore. The widespread belief that the universe consists of three superimposed worlds, the upper or sky world, the middle world of living men and the under world of the dead, is found in a developed form. The upper world is divided into thirteen levels. The uppermost four levels are called *Teteocan*, the abode of the gods, and are considered to be invisible. The creator of all, Ometeuctli, Lord of Duality, dwells with his spouse in the highest heaven and under him in order are the Place of the Red God of Fire, the Place of the Yellow Sun God and the Place of the White Evening Star God. The inferior heavens, called *Ilhuicatl*, are given over to the visible celestial activities. There is one heaven for the storms, another for the blue sky of the day, the dark sky of the night, the comets, the evening star, the sun, the stars, etc.

The under world is *Mictlan*, the Place of the Dead. Nine divisions are commonly given and in the lowermost of these lives *Mictlanteuctli*, the Lord of

Death, and his mate. The idea of future blessing or punishment is not entirely absent from the minds of the Aztecs. Warriors killed in battle go to the House of the Sun, in one of the upper worlds, as do women who die in childbirth. *Tlalocan,* the lowermost heaven, is a sort of terrestrial paradise for others. *Mictlan* is, however, the common abode of the dead, and the wretched soul can reach it only after a journey set with horrors.

The cult of the quarters is intimately associated with the concept of the universe. With the four cardinal points a number of others are sometimes taken including the zenith, the nadir, and the middle. The sacred numbers 4, 5, 6, and 7 may thus conceivably be derived from the points of space, but it would be very unsafe to assume that they are necessarily so derived. The general concept of a universe divided into quarters, fifths, or sixths is a powerful conventionalizing factor in mythology, religion, and art. Prayers, songs, and important acts are repeated in identical or in systematically varied form for each point of space. In Mayan and Aztecan codices the symbolism of the four directions is often manifest.

Ceremonies. Ceremonialism was intensely developed in Mexico and the dramatic quality of many Aztecan rites of human sacrifice has probably never been equaled. We are apt to think only of the gruesome features of human sacrifice and to overlook the spiritual ones. The victim was often regarded as a personification of a god and as such he was fêted, clothed in fine garments, and given every honor. Efforts were made to cause the victim to go willingly to his death uplifted by a truly religious ecstasy. It was considered unlucky that he should grieve or falter.

The religious calendar was given over to fixed and movable feasts. The fixed feasts were eighteen in number and each came on the last day of a twenty-day period and gave its name to that period. These eighteen periods correspond with the Mayan uinals or months, but since dates were rarely given in relation to them, they do not have the same calendrical importance. The five days that rounded out the 365-day year were considered unlucky.

Each of the eighteen feasts of the year was under the patronage of a special divinity and each had a set of ceremonies all its own. In some cases the ceremonies were really culminations of long periods of preparation. Thus, on the last day of the month Toxcatl there was sacrificed a young man, chosen from captured chieftains for his beauty and accomplishments, who for an entire year had been fitting himself for his one turn on the stage of blood and death. This intended victim, gayly attired and accompanied by a retinue of pages, was granted the freedom of the city. When the month of Toxcatl entered he was given brides, whose names were those of goddesses, and in his honor was held a succession of brilliant festivals. On the last day there was a parade of canoes across Lake Texcoco and when a certain piece of desert land was reached, the brides and courtiers bade farewell to the victim. His pages accompanied him by a little-used trail to the base of an apparently ruined temple. Here he was stripped of his splendid garments and of the jewels that were symbols of divinity. With only a necklace of flutes he mounted the steps of the pyramid. At each step he broke one of the flutes and he arrived at the summit, where the priests waited, knife in hand, a naked man whose heart was to be offered to the very god he had impersonated. This ceremony is given only as an example, but it illustrates two characteristics that are seen in several other sacrifices, namely, the paying of homage and honor to the intended sacrificial victim, and, secondly, the necessity of keeping the victim in a happy frame of mind.

The eleventh feast of the year was called Ochpaniztli, "the feast of the broom" and was celebrated in honor of the goddess known as Toci, or Teteoinnan. The first of these names means "our female ancestor" and the second one means "the mother of the gods." She was a goddess of the earth and her symbol was the grass broom with which the earth was swept. She also exerted an influence over the arts of the hearth, such as weaving. Her pictures in the codices show her with a broom in one hand and a shield in the other while about her head is a band of unspun cotton into which are stuck spindles wrapped with thread.

During this month the roads were repaired, the houses and plazas swept, and the temples and idols refurbished. According to the text in the Codex Magliabecchiano there were human sacrifices in the temples which fronted on the roads and there were great dances and carousals. Those sacrificed were afterwards flayed as in the feast of Xipe and their skins worn by dancers. The picture that accompanies this revolting admission is itself devoid of any morbid symbols. It shows a kneeling woman holding out the broom and shield. She wears a white dress and a neckless of jade beads with golden bells for pendants. Below her are two standing men who bear in their hands offerings of ripe fruit.

Sahagun gives details of a terrible drama that was enacted during this twenty-day month. For the first eight days there was dancing without song and without the drum. After this prologue a woman was chosen to impersonate the patron goddess and to wear her characteristic dress and ornaments. With her was a retinue of women skilled in medicine and midwifery. For four days these persons divided in opposing ranks and pelted each other with leaves and flowers. While this harmless ceremony and others like it were being acted out, the greatest care was taken that the woman who played the rôle of the goddess and who was marked for death should not suspect her fate. It was considered unlucky, indeed, if this victim wept or was sad. When her time to die had come she was clothed in rich garments and given to understand that she should be that night the bride of a rich lord. And under such a beguiling belief she was led silently to the temple of sacrifice. There without warning an attendant lifted her upon himself, back to back, and her head was instantly struck off. Without delay the skin was stripped from her warm body and a youth, wearing it as a garment, was conducted in the midst of captives to the temple of the War God, Huitzilopochtli. Here in the presence of this mighty god the youth himself tore out the hearts of four victims and then abandoned the rest to the knife of the head priest. Thus closed the terrible drama which began with an innocent battle of flowers and ended in an orgy of blood.

The twelfth month passed under two names. It was called Pachtli after a plant with which the temples were decorated and Teotleco which signifies "the arrival of the gods." The principal feast was held, as usual, on the twentieth day when the great company of gods was supposed to return from a far land. One god, very youthful and robust, arrived on the eighteenth day, being able to outwalk the others, while a few very old and infirm divinities were late in getting to the feast. The one who arrived first was called Telpochtli or Titlacauan but in reality he was the great Tezcatlipoca in disguise.

In anticipation of this return, the temples, shrines, and household idols were decorated with branches. The youths who did this work were repaid in corn, the amount varying from a full basket to a few ears. A novel manner of attesting the earliest presence of divinity is related. Some cornmeal was spread in a circular mass upon the ground. During the night the high priests kept vigil and from time to time visited this circle of cornmeal. When he saw a footprint in the center he cried out, "Our master has come." Then there was a burst of music and everyone ran to the great feast in the temple. Much native wine was drunk, for this was considered equivalent to washing the tired feet of the travel-worn gods. As a final act of the celebration there was a dance in costume around a great fire and several unfortunates were tossed alive into the flames.

Space will not permit a further examination of the eighteen fixed feasts. The movable feasts were mostly in definite relation to the *tonalamatl* and were thus subject to repetition every 260 days. The permutation of twenty day names and thirteen numbers is pictured in Mexican codices in two or more stereotyped forms, but these are very complete. In the commonest form the entire cycle is divided into twenty groups of thirteen days each and each group is presided over by a special divinity. There are other repeating series of gods, sacred birds, etc., that preside over the individual days in these groups. The *tonalamatl* was much used in Mexico in connection with foretelling events. The days were lucky, indifferent, or unlucky, and the future life of a child was believed to be locked up in the horoscope of his birthday.

Other feasts were held in relation to longer time periods. There were important festivals held in connection with the planet Venus with especially elaborate ones falling at intervals of eight years. Still another ceremony was held at the completion of a fifty-two year period, when the set of years were figuratively bundled up and laid away and a new sacred fire lighted.

Poetry and Music. The languages of Central America were capable of considerable literary development. This is seen especially in the songs that were used in different religious ceremonies of the Aztecs, as well as in the reflective poems written by educated natives. Several very fine pieces have been preserved, and while there is no rhyme, there is much rhythm. When recited by a person speaking fluently the native tongue these poems are very impressive. Of course, translation is always hazardous, and fundamental differences in language, such as exist between English and Aztecan, make it almost impossible. The most famous poet whose name has come down to us was Nezahualcoyotl, or Famishing Coyote, who was a ruler of Texcoco and died at the advanced age of eighty years in 1472. A few verses from one of his poems on the mutability of life and the certainty of death have been translated as follows:—

All the earth is a grave, and naught escapes it; nothing is so perfect that it does not fall and disappear. The rivers, brooks, fountains and waters flow on, and never return to their joyous beginnings; they hasten on to the vast realms of Tlaloc, and the wider they spread between their marges the more rapidly do they mould their own sepulchral urns. That which was yesterday is not today; and let not that which is today trust to live tomorrow.

The caverns of earth are filled with pestilential dust which once was the bones, the flesh, the bodies of great ones who sat upon thrones, deciding causes, ruling assemblies, governing armies, conquering provinces, possessing treasures, tearing down temples, flattering themselves with pride, majesty, fortune, praise and dominion. These glories have passed like the dark smoke thrown out by the fires of Popocatepetl, leaving no monuments but the rude skins on which they are written.

Another example will serve to emphasize the strain of sadness and the vision of death that characterize so many Aztecan poems.

Sad and strange it is to see and reflect on the prosperity and power of the old and dying king Tezozomoc; watered with ambition and avarice, he grew like a willow tree rising above the grass and flowers of spring, rejoicing for a long time, until at length withered and decayed, the storm wind of death tore him from his roots and dashing him in fragments to the ground. The same fate befell the ancient King Colzatzli, so that no memory was left of him, nor of his lineage.

The Aztecs held concerts in the open air where poems were sung to the accompaniment of the drum and other simple instruments. Songs were also sung at banquets and in the stress of love and war. The common musical instruments of the Aztecs vary but little from those in use elsewhere in Mexico and Central America. There were two kinds of drums. One was a horizontal hollowed-out log with an

H-shaped cutting made longitudinally on its upper surface so as to form two vibrating strips which were struck with wooden drumsticks having tips of rubber. The second sort of drum was an upright log also hollowed out and covered with a drumhead of deerskin. Conches were used for trumpets. Resonator whistles with or without finger holes

Fig. 81. A Mexican Orchestra: 1, log drum; 2, kettle drum; 3–4, flageolets; 5, gourd rattle; 6, turtle shell. Manuscrit du Cacique.

were made of clay in fanciful shapes. Flageolets were constructed of clay, bone, or wood and flutes were made of reed. Resounding metal disks and tortoise shells were beaten in time. Many sorts of gourd and earthenware rattles were employed as well as notched bones which were rasped with a scraping stick. Copper bells of the sleigh bell type were exceedingly common. The marimba, however, that is such a favorite musical instrument today in Central America is of African origin and fairly recent introduction. No stringed instruments were known to the ancient Mexicans nor does the pan-pipe appear to have been used in this area although common in Peru.

Minor Aztecan Arts. Some of the great sculptures of Tenochtitlan have already been described and references have been made to the native books painted in brilliant colors on paper and deerskin. Objects of minor art comprise pottery vessels, ornaments of gold, silver, copper, jade, and other precious materials, textiles, pieces of feather work, etc.

The best known ceramic products are made of orange colored clay and carry designs in black that sometimes are realistic, but more often not. The tripod dishes with the bottoms roughed by cross scoring were used to grind chili. Heavy bowls with loop handles on the sides and a channel across the bottom were seemingly made to be strung on ropes. They may have held pitch and been used for street lights. The pottery figurines of the Aztecan period are nearly all moulded and lack the sharp detail of the earlier examples. They often represent deities wearing characteristic dress and carrying ceremonial objects.

Comparatively few specimens of ancient gold work in Mexico escaped the cupidity of the Spanish conquerors, but these attest a remarkable proficiency in casting. The moulds were made of clay mixed with ground charcoal and the melting of gold was accomplished by means of a blow pipe. The technique seen in Costa Rican gold work according to which details falsely appear to be added by soldered wire, was followed in Mexico. Modern Mexican filigree bears little relation to the ancient Indian work, but is probably of Moorish origin. The examples of Aztecan gold work include finger rings, earrings, nose and lip ornaments, necklaces, and pendants.

Among the precious and semi-precious stones known to the Aztecs, the most valuable in their eyes was turquoise. This was probably obtained by trade from the Pueblo Indians. It was mostly cut into thin plates and used in the manufacture of mosaic objects. Red jasper, green jade, jet, gold, and shell of various colors was also used in these mosaics. Jade was highly prized and was known as *chalchihuitl*. Ornaments

of obsidian, a black volcanic glass, and of crystal quartz, are fairly common and others of opal and amethyst have been found. Pearls and emeralds were secured in trade from the south.

The textile decorations in vogue at the coming of the Spaniards can be restored from the pictures in codices. Mantles were

Fig. 82. Mexican Blanket with the Design that represents interlacing Sand and Water called "Spider Water."

often demanded as tribute and the designs are given on the conventional bundles in the tribute lists. Garments with certain designs served as insignia of office for several of the priesthoods. Feather mosaic was highly prized and was made according to several methods. Capes as well as shields and

other objects were covered with brilliant feathers
so arranged as to bring out designs in the natural
colors.

The Tarascans. The Aztecs while by far the most
important tribe in the fifteenth century did not dom-
inate all the surrounding peoples. For instance,
most of the State of Michoacan was controlled by
the Tarascan tribe who defeated every expedition
sent against them. The list of Tarascan towns is
a long one but Tzintzuntzan which means the
"Place of the Humming Birds" was the capital and
principal stronghold. The ancient history of the
Tarascans is little known. Large and striking
specimens of archaic art were formerly accredited
to this people, but without good reason. It is likely
that archaic characters in art were maintained in
Michoacan after they had passed away in central
Mexico, but we cannot be sure that the Tarascans
were the ancient inhabitants. There is some evidence, however, of culture which can be associated
with them. The peculiar T-shaped mounds called
yatacas, which rise in terraces and are faced with
stone slabs laid without mortar, may have been
built by this tribe. Sculptures of rather fine quality
are occasionally found, an example being a reclining
god of the type made famous by the "Chacmool" of
Chichen Itza. Many fine copper celts have been
unearthed in this highly mineralized mountain region. When the Spaniards came the Tarascans
were skilled in weaving and were particularly famous for feather mosaics and feather pictures made
largely of the brilliant plumage of humming birds.
The use of the *atlatl* or spear-thrower survives
among the present-day Indians who also make

gourd vessels covered with colored clays in pleasing geometric and floral designs.

The Otomis are a tribe of central Mexico even less cultured than the Tarascans and there is some evidence that they entered this region from the south only a few centuries before the Spaniards. Their relatives, the Matlatzincas of the Valley of Toluca, had more interesting arts.

Southern Mexico. Somewhere about the middle of the fifteenth century Moctezuma I planted an Aztecan colony at Uaxyacac on the edge of the Zapotecan territory to protect the trade route to Tabasco. This name gave rise to the modern Oaxaca. From this point expeditions were sent out which harrassed the Zapotecs to the south and the Mixtecs to the west. In the Tribute Roll of Mocte-

Fig. 83. The Year Symbol of southern Mexico. It is combined with the four year bearers, House, Rabbit, Reed, and Stone. In the second detail the day 6 Serpent in the year 12 Rabbit is recorded.

zuma II more than twenty Zapotecan towns are listed as paying tribute that consisted of gold disks and gold dust, jadeite beads, quetzal feathers, cochineal dye, fine textiles, etc. Very little is preserved concerning the traditional history of southern Mexico, but it is presumed that the Zapotecan culture before the Aztecan ascendency was a development of that implanted many centuries before when Monte Alban flourished and which we have already examined. As for the Mixtecs we only know that they produced pottery of great beauty somewhat similar to that of Cholula.

Fig. 84. Year Bearers in the Codex Porfirio Diaz ascribed to the Cuicatecan tribe: Wind, Deer, Herb, and Movement.

Some of the finest pre-Cortesian codices that have come down to us are probably of Zapotecan and Mixtecan origin although reflecting to some extent the religion of the Aztecs. Several of these have been interpreted by Doctor Seler in terms of Aztecan religion and art. Among the documents from southern Mexico that belong to the late period are:—

Codex Borgia
Codex Vaticanus 3773
Codex Bologna

Codex Féjervary-Mayer
Codex Vindobonensis
Codex Nuttall or Zouche

Several *lienzos* or documents written on cloth are also from this region. The Lienzo of Amoltepec which is a fine example of this class is conserved in the American Museum of Natural History. The documents from southern Mexico are distinguished by details of geometric ornament that resemble the panels of geometric design on the temples of Mitla.

They record historical events, give astronomical information and present much pictographic evidence on various ceremonies and religious usages. In giving a date a somewhat different method is used than we have seen in the historical records from the Valley of Mexico. There is a definite year sign (Fig. 83) and with it is combined the year bearer,

Fig. 85. A Page from the Codex Nuttall, recording the Conquest of a Town situated on an Island of the Sea. The conquerors come in boats and the conquest is indicated by a spear thrust into the place name hieroglyph. The crocodile, flying fish, and the sea serpent are represented in the water.

or initial day of the year, and often the particular day of the event. Unfortunately, this is not entirely satisfactory because no month signs are recorded and a day with a certain name and number frequently occurs twice in one year. The year

bearers are the same as among the Aztecs for most of the documents, namely, Knife, House, Rabbit, and Reed, but in a manuscript ascribed to a tribe in southern Mexico called the Cuicatecs, the year bearers are Wind, Deer, Herb, and Movement (Fig. 84). Conquest of a town is shown by a spear thrust into the place name. Individuals are often named after the day on which they were born. Thus 8 Deer is a warrior hero in the Codex Nuttall and 3 Knife is a woman who also plays a prominent part. In some of the manuscripts from southern Mexico we see details that are very close to those in the codices of the Mayas.

Fig. 86. The God Macuilxochitl, Five Flower, as shown in a Mexican Codex and in Pottery from southern Mexico.

Aztecan Influence in Central America. The influence from the late Mexican cultures can be traced far to the south.

Decorative motives that show affiliations to those of the Aztecs and their immediate predecessors are found as far south as Costa Rica but the strain is thin and not to be compared with the evidences of culture connection over wide territories that are found on earlier horizons. There was clearly a brisk trade in gold in Aztecan times between the Isthmus of Panama and Mexico.

After the breakdown of the civilization of the humid lands of Central America, following the Mayan cataclysm, the abandoned regions appear to have been repopulated by a stream of tribes from South America who swept up the coast of the Caribbean Sea and across the peninsula of Yucatan, as far as Tehuantepec. There was also a strong northern movement of tribes along the Pacific Coast seen most clearly in the distribution of languages belonging to the Chiapanecan or Chorotegan stock. The early historic records show the Mazateca in transit from their old home in Costa Rica to their new one in northern Oaxaca. Cortez in 1526 found these Indians in Yucatan.

A Cross-Section of New World History

This survey of ancient history in Mexico and Central America discloses a condition which doubtless holds true of the archæological record in other parts of the world. The earliest sedentary culture was by far the most homogeneous and widespread. This means it modified slowly and lasted for ages. At the same time, owing to the connection of the archaic complex with agriculture, the initial spread may have been rapid. The plants domesticated by the American Indians were developed far beyond the wild types, much farther indeed, than the domestic plants of the Old World. This development must have extended over many centuries. The first horizon of agriculture was based on plants of an arid highland environment. The second horizon of agriculture was based on these same plants after they had been slowly modified to fit a humid lowland environment, as well as on certain new plants of humid lowland origin.

The Mayan civilization was specialized to the wet lowlands of the tropic zone and while the influence exerted by this dominant culture of the New World was felt over a great area, the exact characters were not reproduced elsewhere. Trade relations can be traced from Yucatan to Colombia on the one hand and on the other to New Mexico. The cycle of the Mayan civilization was comparatively short and the cycles of the resultant civilizations were even shorter. All New World history must be referred ultimately to the horizons of culture described above, with the standard chronology of the Mayas as the only definite scale.

In the cross-section of New World history presented herewith the horizontal measures represent space and the vertical measures represent time. The line A–B–C–D begins at Victoria Island and ends at Cape Horn, cutting across the culture areas named on the diagram. Over a large part of this cross-section the "horizon of recorded history" is in fact the time of the first European exploration, but in Colombia and Peru, there are well-defined traditions giving lists of kings, while in Central America there is exact chronology going back 2000 years before the coming of the white man. Below this and within it there are archæological records of culture sequence which in some regions, such as the Pueblo Area, have been nicely classified. On the basis of trade relations and diffused ideas in material and esthetic arts the marginal chronology can be tied in with that of the central standard section of history. Of course, all dates earlier than the first recorded ones are theoretical. The beginning of agriculture in America is put at 4000 B. C.—it may be earlier, but can hardly be much later.

In the Pueblo or Southwest Area a single type of flint corn, doubtless introduced from the south, appears on the first agricultural level. Contacts with Mexico and Central America are inferable during Basket Maker II and III, the latter stratum having female fetishes roughly comparable with those of the Archaic Horizon of Mexico. Later Southwest evolution is autochthonous until the end of Pueblo III when the concepts of the Plumed Serpent, the Eagle Man, Four-direction symbolism, etc., come from Mexico with Toltec trade. Culture sequence in the Southwest is about as follows:—

Pueblo V	Modern	1692 to present time
Pueblo IVb	Early Historic	1538 to 1692
Pueblo IVa	Protohistoric	1200 to 1538
Pueblo IIIb	Toltec Trade	1000 to 1200
Pueblo IIIa	Urban Developments	
Pueblo II	Small House	
Pueblo I	Proto-Pueblo	
Basket Maker III	First Pottery	
Basket Maker II	First Agriculture	
Basket Maker I	Nomadic	

In Colombia, Ecuador, and Peru culture successions are now being worked out. The best criterion of age is found in metals which enter Central America from South America after the fall of the First Mayan Empire, i.e., after 630 A. D. The technology of metal working is continuous from southern Colombia to central Mexico. Negative painting with wax has a wider and perhaps earlier distribution, reaching Ecuador and Peru in association with tripod pottery which is otherwise rare in the Andean region. Various motives of design link the two continents, especially on the Toltec-Chorotegan level. Between 1000 and 1200 A. D. civilization seems to have been generally stabilized, but this halcyon age was followed by disorganization and far-reaching migrations. The pre-Spanish horizons of southern Peru are tentatively arranged as follows by A. L. Kroeber, the apparently earlier material of Ancon being omitted for lack of the cross-ties.

> III.   Inca
> IIc. Late Ica
> IIb. Middle Ica
> IIa. Epigonal
> Ib.   Late Nasca
> Ia.   Early Nasca

The early Nasca civilization was far from primitive being characterized by pyramids, fine textiles, and some metal. Mayan strains have been recognized in Chavin and Recuay in Peru and various sites in Ecuador.

The dynamic forces in the history of man in the New World have a tremendous bearing upon the present and future state of the world. The debt which we owe to the ancient civilizations of Mexico and Central America becomes apparent when we list the more important agricultural plants, fibers, gums, dyes, etc., which were taken over by Europeans from the American Indians.

Food Plants Cultivated by American Indians

Maize	Pineapples	Cashew nut
Potatoes	Nispero	Jocote
Sweet potatoes	Barbados cherry	Star apples
Tomatoes	Strawberries	Paraguay tea
Pumpkins	Persimmons	Alligator pear
Squashes	Papaws	Chirimoya
Lima beans	Guava	Sour sop
Kidney beans	Arracacha	Sweet sop
Peppers	Peanuts	Custard apple
Cacao	Oca	Cassava

Important Economic Contributions of American Indians

FIBERS

Cotton
Henequen
Pita

MEDICINES

Tobacco
Cinchona (Quinine)
Cascara Sagrada
Cocaine
Ipecac
Sarsaparilla

DOMESTICATED ANIMALS

Alpaca
Llama
Guinea pig
Dog (perhaps Old World)
Muscovy duck
Turkey

GUMS

Rubber
Copal
Peruvian Balsam
Chicle

DYES

Añil (Indigo)
Cochineal
Logwood
Fustic

Diagram of American Chronology

Column headers: A | ARCTIC | CANADIAN FOREST | GREAT PLAINS | SOUTHWEST | B | CENTRAL MEXICAN | MAYAN | COLOMBIAN | AMAZON FOREST | C | PERUVIAN | SOUTHERN PLAINS | SOUTHERN FOREST | D

Time scale: AD 1900 · 1500 · 1000 · 500 · 0 · BC 500 · 1000 · 1500 · 2000 · 2500 · 3000 · 3500 · 4000 · 5000 · 6000 · 7000

HISTORY — RECORDED

HORIZON OF

Southwest: Pueblo V, Pueblo IV, Pueblo III, Pueblo II, Pueblo I, Basket Maker III, Basket Maker II, Basket Maker I

Central Mexican: Aztec, Toltec, Zapotec, Totonac, Upper Archaic, Middle Archaic, Lower Archaic

Mayan: Second Empire, Transition, First Empire, Day Count, Chorotegan

Colombian: Chibcha, Quimbaya

Peruvian: Inca, Ica, Epigonal, Nasca, Ancon Shell Heaps

SECOND HORIZON OF AGRICULTURE (HUMID)

FIRST HORIZON OF AGRICULTURE (ARID)

Primary Distribution of Agriculture, Pottery and Loom Weaving

Invention of Agriculture

NOMADIC, NON-AGRICULTURAL HORIZON
(Survives, till present time in marginal areas)

Primary Invasion from Asia via Alaska on upper Paleolithic or lower Neolithic, without agriculture, pottery or loom weaving. 15000—10000 BC.

BIBLIOGRAPHY

A brief list of books on Mexico and Central America is appended. These books may be consulted in the Museum Library as well as others referred to in the more complete bibliographies that will be found in the works cited.

BANCROFT, H. H. *The Native Races of the Pacific States.* 5 vols. New York and London, 1875–1876.

BANDELIER, ADOLPH F. *On the Distribution and Tenure of Lands and the Customs with Respect to Inheritance, among the Ancient Mexicans.* (Eleventh Annual Report, Peabody Museum of American Archæology and Ethnology, vol. 2, no. 2, pp. 384–448, Cambridge, 1878.)

Social Organization and Mode of Government of the Ancient Mexicans. (Twelfth Annual Report, Peabody Museum of American Archæology and Ethnology, vol. 2, no. 3, Cambridge, 1879.)

BOWDITCH, C. P. *The Numeration, Calendar Systems and Astronomical Knowledge of the Mayas.* Cambridge, 1910.

BRANSFORD, J. F. *Archæological Researches in Nicaragua.* (Smithsonian Contributions to Knowledge, XXV, Art. 2, pp. 1–96, 1881.)

BRINTON, D. G. *The Maya Chronicles.* Philadelphia, 1882. (No. 1 of Brinton's Library of Aboriginal American Literature.)

The Annals of the Cakchiquels. The original text with a translation, notes and introduction. Philadelphia, 1885. (No. 6 of Brinton's Library of Aboriginal American Literature.)

Essays of an Americanist. Philadelphia, 1890.

BULLETIN 28. *Mexican and Central American Antiquities, Calendar Systems and History.* Twenty-four papers by Eduard Seler, E. Förstemann, Paul Schellhas, Carl Sapper and E. P. Dieseldorff. Translated from the German under the supervision of Charles P. Bowditch. (Bulletin 28, Bureau of American Ethnology, Washington, 1904.)

CHARNAY, D. *The Ancient Cities of the New World.* Trans. by J. Gonino and H. S. Conant. London, 1887.

DIAS DEL CASTILLO, BERNAL. *The True History of the Conquest of Mexico, 1568.* 3 vols. (Translated by A. P. Maudslay. Hakluyt Society, London, 1908.)

255

FÖRSTEMANN, E. *Commentary of the Maya Manuscript in the Royal Public Library of Dresden.* (Papers, Peabody Museum, IV, No. 2, pp. 48–266, 1906.)

GANN, T. *Mounds in Northern Honduras.* (Nineteenth Annual Report, Bureau of American Ethnology, part 2, pp. 661–692, Washington, 1897–1898.)

HARTMANN, C. V. *Archœological Researches in Costa Rica.* (The Royal Ethnographical Museum in Stockholm, Stockholm, 1901.)
        Archœological Researches on the Pacific Coast of Costa Rica. (Memoirs, Carnegie Institute, vol. 3, pp. 1–95, 1907.)

HOLMES, W. H. *Ancient Art of the Province of Chiriqui.* (Sixth Annual Report, Bureau of American Ethnology, pp. 3–187, Washington, 1888.)
        Archœological Studies among the Ancient Cities in Mexico. (Publications, Field Columbian Museum, Chicago, 1895–1897.)

JOYCE, T. A. *Mexican Archœology.* An Introduction to the Archæology of the Mexican and Maya Civilizations of pre-Spanish America. New York and London, 1914.
        Central American and West Indies Archœology. Being an Introduction to the Archæology of the States of Nicaragua, Costa Rica, Panama and the West Indies. New York, 1916.
        Maya and Mexican Art. London, 1927.

KINGSBOROUGH, LORD. *Antiquities of Mexico.* 9 vols., folio. London, 1831–1848.

LEHMANN, W. *Methods and Results in Mexican Research.* Trans. by Seymour de Ricci. Paris, 1909.
        Ergebnisse einer Forschungsreise in Mittelamerika und Mexico 1907–1909. (Zeitschrift für Ethnologie, Band 42, pp. 687–749, 1910.)
        Zentral Amerika. Die Sprachen Zentral-Amerikas in ihren Beziehungen zueinander sowie zu Süd-Amerika und Mexiko. In zwei Banden. Band 1. Berlin, 1920.

LOTHROP, S. K. *Pottery of Costa Rica and Nicaragua.* (Contributions, Museum of the American Indian, Heye Foundation, vol. VIII, 1926.)

LUMHOLTZ, C. *Unknown Mexico.* 2 vols. New York, 1902.
        Symbolism of the Huichol Indians. (Memoirs, American Museum of Natural History, vol. 3, part 1, 1900.)
        Decorative Art of the Huichol Indians. (Memoirs, American Museum of Natural History, vol. 3, part 4, 1904.)

MacCURDY, G. G. *A Study of Chiriquian Antiquities.* (Memoirs, Connecticut Academy of Sciences, vol. 3, 1911.)

MAUDSLAY, A. P. *Biologia Centrali-Americana, or Contributions to the Knowledge of the Flora and Fauna of Mexico and Central America. Archæology,* 4 vols. of text and plates. London, 1889–1902.

MEMOIRS OF THE PEABODY MUSEUM, vols. 1–5. Reports on excavations and exploration by Gordon, Maler, Thompson, and Tozzer.

MORLEY, S. G. *An Introduction to the Study of the Maya Hieroglyphs.* (Bulletin 57, Bureau of American Ethnology, Washington, 1915.)

    The Inscriptions at Copan. (Publication 219, Carnegie Institution of Washington, Washington, 1920.)

PEÑAFIEL, A. *Monumentos del arte Mexicano antiguo.* 3 vols. Berlin, 1890.

    Nomenclatura geografica de Mexico. Mexico, 1897.

SAHAGUN, BERNARDINO DE. *Histoire générale des Choses de la Nouvelle-Espagne.* (Edited and translated by D. Jourdanet and Rémi Siméon.) 1880.

    Historia de las cosas de Nueva España. (Portfolio of illustrations from two Sahagun manuscripts copied under direction of F. del Paso y Troncoso and issued by the Mexican Government. Florence, 1922.)

SAVILLE, MARSHALL H. *Turquois Mosaic Art in Ancient Mexico.* (Contributions, Museum of the American Indian, Heye Foundation, vol. VI, 1922.)

    The Wood-Carver's Art in Ancient Mexico. (Contributions, Museum of the American Indian, Heye Foundation, vol. IX, 1925.)

SCHELLHAS, P. *Representation of Deities of the Maya Manuscripts.* 2nd edition revised. (Translated by Miss Selma Wesselhoeft and Miss A. M. Parker, Papers, Peabody Museum, vol. 4, No. 1, pp. 7–47, 1904.)

SELER, E. *Die alten Ansiedelungen von Chaculá im Districkte Nenton des Departments Huehuetenango der Republic Guatemala.* Berlin, 1901.

    Gesammelte Abhandlungen zur amerikanischen Sprach- und Alterthumskunde. 5 vols. Berlin, 1908–1923.

    Codex Vaticanus No. 3773 (Codex Vaticanus B). An Old Mexican Pictorial Manuscript in the Vatican Library. (Translated by A. H. Keane.) Berlin and London, 1902–1903.

SPINDEN, H. J.   *A Study of Maya Art.*   Memoirs, Peabody Museum, vol. 6, 1913.)

       The Reduction of Maya Dates.   (Papers, Peabody Museum of American Archæology and Ethnology, Harvard University, vol. 6, no. 4, Cambridge, 1924.)

SQUIER, E. G.   *The States of Central America: their Geography, Topography, Climate, Population,* etc.   New York, 1858.

STEPHENS, J. L.   *Central America, Chiapas and Yucatan.*   2 vols. New York, 1841.

       Incidents of Travel in Yucatan.   2 vols.   New York, 1843.

THOMAS, C.   *A Study of the Manuscript Troano.*   (U. S. Geographical and Geological Survey of the Rocky Mountain Region, Contributions to American Ethnology, V, pp. 1–224, 1882.)

THOMAS, C., AND SWANTON, JOHN R.   *Indian Languages of Mexico and Central America.*   (Bulletin 44, Bureau of American Ethnology, Washington, 1911.)

TOZZER, A. M.   *A Comparative Study of the Mayas and Lacandones.* New York, 1907.

       A Maya Grammar, with Bibliography and Appraisement of the Works Noted.   (Papers, Peabody Museum of American Archæology and Ethnology, Harvard University, vol. 9, Cambridge, 1921.)

INDEX

Acropolis, artificial, 72, 74, 77.

Adobe, 63; houses, Mexican, 15.

Agriculture, connection with archaic art, 249; distribution of, 68, 70, 71; distribution in the New World, 67, 68, 70; influence on Mayan culture, 73; invention of, 45, 51–53, 67, 251; spread and development of, 63, 70, 250.

Ah Puch, Lord of Death, 101.

Alphabet, of Landa, 125.

Altars, Mayan, 84; Quirigua, 108.

Amulets, archaic figurines as, 61; gold, 198.

Animals, domestication of, 20, 59, 253.

Annals of Quauhtitlan, 171, 172.

Arch, in Mayan architecture, 79.

Archaic, art, 45–46, 53–57, 58, 75, 244; art, on borders of Mayan area, 75; art, local developments of, 63–68; culture, 187, 249; culture, distribution of, 63–66, 69; culture, figures, 60, 61, 62; figurines, 53–57; horizon, 45–71; horizon, extensions of, 63–68; pottery, 46, 59–61; sites, 50; stone sculptures, 61–63.

Architecture, early period of the Mayas, 146; great period of the Mayas, 147; historical sequence determined by, 108–109; Mayan, 77–83; Mitla, 157, 163–164; Monte Alban, 159; period of the League of Mayapan, 149; transition period, Mayan, 148; types of, La Quemada, 182–183; Zapotecan, 159.

Art, archaic, 45–46, 53–57, 75, 244; archaic, characterization of, 53; archaic, Colombia, and Venezuela, 66–67; archaic, local developments of, 63–68; bat, represented in, 20; Chorotegan, 190–195; decorative, Isthmian region, 64, 66; high development of Mayan, 73; massive sculptural, 83–84; Mayan, 89, 146, 147, 148, 149, 150; Mayan, human figure in, 93–94; Mayan, sequences in, 106–109; Mayan, serpent in, 89–93; motives, Huichol, 37–38; Santa Lucia Cozumalhualpa, 188; Tarascan, 244–245; Toltecan, influenced by Mayan, 169, 170; Totonacan, close correspondence to Mayan, 165, 166, 167; Zapotecan, influenced by Mayan, 159.

Arts, minor, Aztecan, 242–244; Mayan, 87–89.

Astronomical, base line, Copan, 138; checks, on correlation with Christian chronology, 136–137; observatories, Mayan, 137–139.

Astronomy, Mayan knowledge of, 73, 111, 133.

Atlatl, 58, 244.

Atzcapotzalco, 203, 204, 209; stratification at, 47–48, 169.

Aztecan history, 204–209.

259

A CATALOG OF SELECTED
DOVER BOOKS
IN ALL FIELDS OF INTEREST

A CATALOG OF SELECTED DOVER
BOOKS IN ALL FIELDS OF INTEREST

CONCERNING THE SPIRITUAL IN ART, Wassily Kandinsky. Pioneering work by father of abstract art. Thoughts on color theory, nature of art. Analysis of earlier masters. 12 illustrations. 80pp. of text. 5⅜ x 8½.   23411-8 Pa. $4.95

ANIMALS: 1,419 Copyright-Free Illustrations of Mammals, Birds, Fish, Insects, etc., Jim Harter (ed.). Clear wood engravings present, in extremely lifelike poses, over 1,000 species of animals. One of the most extensive pictorial sourcebooks of its kind. Captions. Index. 284pp. 9 x 12.   23766-4 Pa. $14.95

CELTIC ART: The Methods of Construction, George Bain. Simple geometric techniques for making Celtic interlacements, spirals, Kells-type initials, animals, humans, etc. Over 500 illustrations. 160pp. 9 x 12. (USO)   22923-8 Pa. $9.95

AN ATLAS OF ANATOMY FOR ARTISTS, Fritz Schider. Most thorough reference work on art anatomy in the world. Hundreds of illustrations, including selections from works by Vesalius, Leonardo, Goya, Ingres, Michelangelo, others. 593 illustrations. 192pp. 7⅛ x 10¼.   20241-0 Pa. $9.95

CELTIC HAND STROKE-BY-STROKE (Irish Half-Uncial from "The Book of Kells"): An Arthur Baker Calligraphy Manual, Arthur Baker. Complete guide to creating each letter of the alphabet in distinctive Celtic manner. Covers hand position, strokes, pens, inks, paper, more. Illustrated. 48pp. 8¼ x 11.   24336-2 Pa. $3.95

EASY ORIGAMI, John Montroll. Charming collection of 32 projects (hat, cup, pelican, piano, swan, many more) specially designed for the novice origami hobbyist. Clearly illustrated easy-to-follow instructions insure that even beginning papercrafters will achieve successful results. 48pp. 8¼ x 11.   27298-2 Pa. $3.50

THE COMPLETE BOOK OF BIRDHOUSE CONSTRUCTION FOR WOODWORKERS, Scott D. Campbell. Detailed instructions, illustrations, tables. Also data on bird habitat and instinct patterns. Bibliography. 3 tables. 63 illustrations in 15 figures. 48pp. 5¼ x 8½.   24407-5 Pa. $2.50

BLOOMINGDALE'S ILLUSTRATED 1886 CATALOG: Fashions, Dry Goods and Housewares, Bloomingdale Brothers. Famed merchants' extremely rare catalog depicting about 1,700 products: clothing, housewares, firearms, dry goods, jewelry, more. Invaluable for dating, identifying vintage items. Also, copyright-free graphics for artists, designers. Co-published with Henry Ford Museum & Greenfield Village. 160pp. 8¼ x 11.   25780-0 Pa. $10.95

HISTORIC COSTUME IN PICTURES, Braun & Schneider. Over 1,450 costumed figures in clearly detailed engravings–from dawn of civilization to end of 19th century. Captions. Many folk costumes. 256pp. 8⅜ x 11¾.   23150-X Pa. $12.95

CATALOG OF DOVER BOOKS

STICKLEY CRAFTSMAN FURNITURE CATALOGS, Gustav Stickley and L. & J. G. Stickley. Beautiful, functional furniture in two authentic catalogs from 1910. 594 illustrations, including 277 photos, show settles, rockers, armchairs, reclining chairs, bookcases, desks, tables. 183pp. 6½ x 9¼. 23838-5 Pa. $11.95

AMERICAN LOCOMOTIVES IN HISTORIC PHOTOGRAPHS: 1858 to 1949, Ron Ziel (ed.). A rare collection of 126 meticulously detailed official photographs, called "builder portraits," of American locomotives that majestically chronicle the rise of steam locomotive power in America. Introduction. Detailed captions. xi + 129pp. 9 x 12. 27393-8 Pa. $13.95

AMERICA'S LIGHTHOUSES: An Illustrated History, Francis Ross Holland, Jr. Delightfully written, profusely illustrated fact filled survey of over 200 American lighthouses since 1716. History, anecdotes, technological advances, more. 240pp. 8 x 10¾. 25576-X Pa. $12.95

TOWARDS A NEW ARCHITECTURE, Le Corbusier. Pioneering manifesto by founder of "International School." Technical and aesthetic theories, views of industry, economics, relation of form to function, "mass-production split" and much more. Profusely illustrated. 320pp. 6⅛ x 9¼. (USO) 25023-7 Pa. $9.95

HOW THE OTHER HALF LIVES, Jacob Riis. Famous journalistic record, exposing poverty and degradation of New York slums around 1900, by major social reformer. 100 striking and influential photographs. 233pp. 10 x 7⅞. 22012-5 Pa. $11.95

FRUIT KEY AND TWIG KEY TO TREES AND SHRUBS, William M. Harlow. One of the handiest and most widely used identification aids. Fruit key covers 120 deciduous and evergreen species; twig key 160 deciduous species. Easily used. Over 300 photographs. 126pp. 5⅜ x 8½. 20511-8 Pa. $3.95

COMMON BIRD SONGS, Dr. Donald J. Borror. Songs of 60 most common U.S. birds: robins, sparrows, cardinals, bluejays, finches, more—arranged in order of increasing complexity. Up to 9 variations of songs of each species. Cassette and manual 99911-4 $8.95

ORCHIDS AS HOUSE PLANTS, Rebecca Tyson Northen. Grow cattleyas and many other kinds of orchids—in a window, in a case, or under artificial light. 63 illustrations. 148pp. 5⅜ x 8½. 23261-1 Pa. $5.95

MONSTER MAZES, Dave Phillips. Masterful mazes at four levels of difficulty. Avoid deadly perils and evil creatures to find magical treasures. Solutions for all 32 exciting illustrated puzzles. 48pp. 8¼ x 11. 26005-4 Pa. $2.95

MOZART'S DON GIOVANNI (DOVER OPERA LIBRETTO SERIES), Wolfgang Amadeus Mozart. Introduced and translated by Ellen H. Bleiler. Standard Italian libretto, with complete English translation. Convenient and thoroughly portable—an ideal companion for reading along with a recording or the performance itself. Introduction. List of characters. Plot summary. 121pp. 5¼ x 8½. 24944-1 Pa. $3.95

TECHNICAL MANUAL AND DICTIONARY OF CLASSICAL BALLET, Gail Grant. Defines, explains, comments on steps, movements, poses and concepts. 15-page pictorial section. Basic book for student, viewer. 127pp. 5⅜ x 8½. 21843-0 Pa. $4.95

THE CLARINET AND CLARINET PLAYING, David Pino. Lively, comprehensive work features suggestions about technique, musicianship, and musical interpretation, as well as guidelines for teaching, making your own reeds, and preparing for public performance. Includes an intriguing look at clarinet history. "A godsend," The Clarinet, Journal of the International Clarinet Society. Appendixes. 7 illus. 320pp. 5⅜ x 8½. 40270-3 Pa. $9.95

HOLLYWOOD GLAMOR PORTRAITS, John Kobal (ed.). 145 photos from 1926-49. Harlow, Gable, Bogart, Bacall; 94 stars in all. Full background on photographers, technical aspects. 160pp. 8⅜ x 11¼. 23352-9 Pa. $12.95

THE ANNOTATED CASEY AT THE BAT: A Collection of Ballads about the Mighty Casey/Third, Revised Edition, Martin Gardner (ed.). Amusing sequels and parodies of one of America's best-loved poems: Casey's Revenge, Why Casey Whiffed, Casey's Sister at the Bat, others. 256pp. 5⅜ x 8½. 28598-7 Pa. $8.95

THE RAVEN AND OTHER FAVORITE POEMS, Edgar Allan Poe. Over 40 of the author's most memorable poems: "The Bells," "Ulalume," "Israfel," "To Helen," "The Conqueror Worm," "Eldorado," "Annabel Lee," many more. Alphabetic lists of titles and first lines. 64pp. 5$\frac{3}{16}$ x 8¼. 26685-0 Pa. $1.00

PERSONAL MEMOIRS OF U. S. GRANT, Ulysses Simpson Grant. Intelligent, deeply moving firsthand account of Civil War campaigns, considered by many the finest military memoirs ever written. Includes letters, historic photographs, maps and more. 528pp. 6⅛ x 9¼. 28587-1 Pa. $12.95

ANCIENT EGYPTIAN MATERIALS AND INDUSTRIES, A. Lucas and J. Harris. Fascinating, comprehensive, thoroughly documented text describes this ancient civilization's vast resources and the processes that incorporated them in daily life, including the use of animal products, building materials, cosmetics, perfumes and incense, fibers, glazed ware, glass and its manufacture, materials used in the mummification process, and much more. 544pp. 6⅛ x 9¼. (USO) 40446-3 Pa. $16.95

RUSSIAN STORIES/PYCCKNE PACCKA3bl: A Dual-Language Book, edited by Gleb Struve. Twelve tales by such masters as Chekhov, Tolstoy, Dostoevsky, Pushkin, others. Excellent word-for-word English translations on facing pages, plus teaching and study aids, Russian/English vocabulary, biographical/critical introductions, more. 416pp. 5⅜ x 8½. 26244-8 Pa. $9.95

PHILADELPHIA THEN AND NOW: 60 Sites Photographed in the Past and Present, Kenneth Finkel and Susan Oyama. Rare photographs of City Hall, Logan Square, Independence Hall, Betsy Ross House, other landmarks juxtaposed with contemporary views. Captures changing face of historic city. Introduction. Captions. 128pp. 8¼ x 11. 25790-8 Pa. $9.95

AIA ARCHITECTURAL GUIDE TO NASSAU AND SUFFOLK COUNTIES, LONG ISLAND, The American Institute of Architects, Long Island Chapter, and the Society for the Preservation of Long Island Antiquities. Comprehensive, well-researched and generously illustrated volume brings to life over three centuries of Long Island's great architectural heritage. More than 240 photographs with authoritative, extensively detailed captions. 176pp. 8¼ x 11. 26946-9 Pa. $14.95

NORTH AMERICAN INDIAN LIFE: Customs and Traditions of 23 Tribes, Elsie Clews Parsons (ed.). 27 fictionalized essays by noted anthropologists examine religion, customs, government, additional facets of life among the Winnebago, Crow, Zuni, Eskimo, other tribes. 480pp. 6⅛ x 9¼. 27377-6 Pa. $10.95

CATALOG OF DOVER BOOKS

FRANK LLOYD WRIGHT'S DANA HOUSE, Donald Hoffmann. Pictorial essay of residential masterpiece with over 160 interior and exterior photos, plans, elevations, sketches and studies. 128pp. 9¼ x 10¾. 29120-0 Pa. $12.95

THE MALE AND FEMALE FIGURE IN MOTION: 60 Classic Photographic Sequences, Eadweard Muybridge. 60 true-action photographs of men and women walking, running, climbing, bending, turning, etc., reproduced from rare 19th-century masterpiece. vi + 121pp. 9 x 12. 24745-7 Pa. $10.95

1001 QUESTIONS ANSWERED ABOUT THE SEASHORE, N. J. Berrill and Jacquelyn Berrill. Queries answered about dolphins, sea snails, sponges, starfish, fishes, shore birds, many others. Covers appearance, breeding, growth, feeding, much more. 305pp. 5¼ x 8¼. 23366-9 Pa. $9.95

ATTRACTING BIRDS TO YOUR YARD, William J. Weber. Easy-to-follow guide offers advice on how to attract the greatest diversity of birds: birdhouses, feeders, water and waterers, much more. 96pp. 5³⁄₁₆ x 8¼. 28927-3 Pa. $2.50

MEDICINAL AND OTHER USES OF NORTH AMERICAN PLANTS: A Historical Survey with Special Reference to the Eastern Indian Tribes, Charlotte Erichsen-Brown. Chronological historical citations document 500 years of usage of plants, trees, shrubs native to eastern Canada, northeastern U.S. Also complete identifying information. 343 illustrations. 544pp. 6½ x 9¼. 25951-X Pa. $12.95

STORYBOOK MAZES, Dave Phillips. 23 stories and mazes on two-page spreads: Wizard of Oz, Treasure Island, Robin Hood, etc. Solutions. 64pp. 8¼ x 11. 23628-5 Pa. $2.95

AMERICAN NEGRO SONGS: 230 Folk Songs and Spirituals, Religious and Secular, John W. Work. This authoritative study traces the African influences of songs sung and played by black Americans at work, in church, and as entertainment. The author discusses the lyric significance of such songs as "Swing Low, Sweet Chariot," "John Henry," and others and offers the words and music for 230 songs. Bibliography. Index of Song Titles. 272pp. 6½ x 9¼. 40271-1 Pa. $9.95

MOVIE-STAR PORTRAITS OF THE FORTIES, John Kobal (ed.). 163 glamor, studio photos of 106 stars of the 1940s: Rita Hayworth, Ava Gardner, Marlon Brando, Clark Gable, many more. 176pp. 8⅜ x 11¼. 23546-7 Pa. $14.95

BENCHLEY LOST AND FOUND, Robert Benchley. Finest humor from early 30s, about pet peeves, child psychologists, post office and others. Mostly unavailable elsewhere. 73 illustrations by Peter Arno and others. 183pp. 5⅜ x 8½. 22410-4 Pa. $6.95

YEKL and THE IMPORTED BRIDEGROOM AND OTHER STORIES OF YIDDISH NEW YORK, Abraham Cahan. Film Hester Street based on Yekl (1896). Novel, other stories among first about Jewish immigrants on N.Y.'s East Side. 240pp. 5⅜ x 8½. 22427-9 Pa. $6.95

SELECTED POEMS, Walt Whitman. Generous sampling from *Leaves of Grass*. Twenty-four poems include "I Hear America Singing," "Song of the Open Road," "I Sing the Body Electric," "When Lilacs Last in the Dooryard Bloom'd," "O Captain! My Captain!"—all reprinted from an authoritative edition. Lists of titles and first lines. 128pp. 5³⁄₁₆ x 8¼. 26878-0 Pa. $1.00

THE BEST TALES OF HOFFMANN, E. T. A. Hoffmann. 10 of Hoffmann's most important stories: "Nutcracker and the King of Mice," "The Golden Flowerpot," etc. 458pp. 5⅜ x 8½. 21793-0 Pa. $9.95

FROM FETISH TO GOD IN ANCIENT EGYPT, E. A. Wallis Budge. Rich detailed survey of Egyptian conception of "God" and gods, magic, cult of animals, Osiris, more. Also, superb English translations of hymns and legends. 240 illustrations. 545pp. 5⅜ x 8½. 25803-3 Pa. $13.95

FRENCH STORIES/CONTES FRANÇAIS: A Dual-Language Book, Wallace Fowlie. Ten stories by French masters, Voltaire to Camus: "Micromegas" by Voltaire; "The Atheist's Mass" by Balzac; "Minuet" by de Maupassant; "The Guest" by Camus, six more. Excellent English translations on facing pages. Also French-English vocabulary list, exercises, more. 352pp. 5⅜ x 8½. 26443-2 Pa. $9.95

CHICAGO AT THE TURN OF THE CENTURY IN PHOTOGRAPHS: 122 Historic Views from the Collections of the Chicago Historical Society, Larry A. Viskochil. Rare large-format prints offer detailed views of City Hall, State Street, the Loop, Hull House, Union Station, many other landmarks, circa 1904-1913. Introduction. Captions. Maps. 144pp. 9⅜ x 12¼. 24656-6 Pa. $12.95

OLD BROOKLYN IN EARLY PHOTOGRAPHS, 1865-1929, William Lee Younger. Luna Park, Gravesend race track, construction of Grand Army Plaza, moving of Hotel Brighton, etc. 157 previously unpublished photographs. 165pp. 8⅞ x 11¾. 23587-4 Pa. $13.95

THE MYTHS OF THE NORTH AMERICAN INDIANS, Lewis Spence. Rich anthology of the myths and legends of the Algonquins, Iroquois, Pawnees and Sioux, prefaced by an extensive historical and ethnological commentary. 36 illustrations. 480pp. 5⅜ x 8½. 25967-6 Pa. $10.95

AN ENCYCLOPEDIA OF BATTLES: Accounts of Over 1,560 Battles from 1479 B.C. to the Present, David Eggenberger. Essential details of every major battle in recorded history from the first battle of Megiddo in 1479 B.C. to Grenada in 1984. List of Battle Maps. New Appendix covering the years 1967-1984. Index. 99 illustrations. 544pp. 6½ x 9¼. 24913-1 Pa. $16.95

SAILING ALONE AROUND THE WORLD, Captain Joshua Slocum. First man to sail around the world, alone, in small boat. One of great feats of seamanship told in delightful manner. 67 illustrations. 294pp. 5⅜ x 8½. 20326-3 Pa. $6.95

ANARCHISM AND OTHER ESSAYS, Emma Goldman. Powerful, penetrating, prophetic essays on direct action, role of minorities, prison reform, puritan hypocrisy, violence, etc. 271pp. 5⅜ x 8½. 22484-8 Pa. $7.95

MYTHS OF THE HINDUS AND BUDDHISTS, Ananda K. Coomaraswamy and Sister Nivedita. Great stories of the epics; deeds of Krishna, Shiva, taken from puranas, Vedas, folk tales; etc. 32 illustrations. 400pp. 5⅜ x 8½. 21759-0 Pa. $12.95

THE TRAUMA OF BIRTH, Otto Rank. Rank's controversial thesis that anxiety neurosis is caused by profound psychological trauma which occurs at birth. 256pp. 5⅜ x 8½. 27974-X Pa. $7.95

A THEOLOGICO-POLITICAL TREATISE, Benedict Spinoza. Also contains unfinished Political Treatise. Great classic on religious liberty, theory of government on common consent. R. Elwes translation. Total of 421pp. 5⅜ x 8½. 20249-6 Pa. $9.95

CATALOG OF DOVER BOOKS

MY BONDAGE AND MY FREEDOM, Frederick Douglass. Born a slave, Douglass became outspoken force in antislavery movement. The best of Douglass' autobiographies. Graphic description of slave life. 464pp. 5⅜ x 8½. 22457-0 Pa. $8.95

FOLLOWING THE EQUATOR: A Journey Around the World, Mark Twain. Fascinating humorous account of 1897 voyage to Hawaii, Australia, India, New Zealand, etc. Ironic, bemused reports on peoples, customs, climate, flora and fauna, politics, much more. 197 illustrations. 720pp. 5⅜ x 8½. 26113-1 Pa. $15.95

THE PEOPLE CALLED SHAKERS, Edward D. Andrews. Definitive study of Shakers: origins, beliefs, practices, dances, social organization, furniture and crafts, etc. 33 illustrations. 351pp. 5⅜ x 8½. 21081-2 Pa. $8.95

THE MYTHS OF GREECE AND ROME, H. A. Guerber. A classic of mythology, generously illustrated, long prized for its simple, graphic, accurate retelling of the principal myths of Greece and Rome, and for its commentary on their origins and significance. With 64 illustrations by Michelangelo, Raphael, Titian, Rubens, Canova, Bernini and others. 480pp. 5⅜ x 8½. 27584-1 Pa. $9.95

PSYCHOLOGY OF MUSIC, Carl E. Seashore. Classic work discusses music as a medium from psychological viewpoint. Clear treatment of physical acoustics, auditory apparatus, sound perception, development of musical skills, nature of musical feeling, host of other topics. 88 figures. 408pp. 5⅜ x 8½. 21851-1 Pa. $11.95

THE PHILOSOPHY OF HISTORY, Georg W. Hegel. Great classic of Western thought develops concept that history is not chance but rational process, the evolution of freedom. 457pp. 5⅜ x 8½. 20112-0 Pa. $9.95

THE BOOK OF TEA, Kakuzo Okakura. Minor classic of the Orient: entertaining, charming explanation, interpretation of traditional Japanese culture in terms of tea ceremony. 94pp. 5⅜ x 8½. 20070-1 Pa. $3.95

LIFE IN ANCIENT EGYPT, Adolf Erman. Fullest, most thorough, detailed older account with much not in more recent books, domestic life, religion, magic, medicine, commerce, much more. Many illustrations reproduce tomb paintings, carvings, hieroglyphs, etc. 597pp. 5⅜ x 8½. 22632-8 Pa. $12.95

SUNDIALS, Their Theory and Construction, Albert Waugh. Far and away the best, most thorough coverage of ideas, mathematics concerned, types, construction, adjusting anywhere. Simple, nontechnical treatment allows even children to build several of these dials. Over 100 illustrations. 230pp. 5⅜ x 8½. 22947-5 Pa. $8.95

THEORETICAL HYDRODYNAMICS, L. M. Milne-Thomson. Classic exposition of the mathematical theory of fluid motion, applicable to both hydrodynamics and aerodynamics. Over 600 exercises. 768pp. 6⅛ x 9¼. 68970-0 Pa. $20.95

SONGS OF EXPERIENCE: Facsimile Reproduction with 26 Plates in Full Color, William Blake. 26 full-color plates from a rare 1826 edition. Includes "TheTyger," "London," "Holy Thursday," and other poems. Printed text of poems. 48pp. 5¼ x 7. 24636-1 Pa. $4.95

OLD-TIME VIGNETTES IN FULL COLOR, Carol Belanger Grafton (ed.). Over 390 charming, often sentimental illustrations, selected from archives of Victorian graphics—pretty women posing, children playing, food, flowers, kittens and puppies, smiling cherubs, birds and butterflies, much more. All copyright-free. 48pp. 9¼ x 12¼. 27269-9 Pa. $7.95

PERSPECTIVE FOR ARTISTS, Rex Vicat Cole. Depth, perspective of sky and sea, shadows, much more, not usually covered. 391 diagrams, 81 reproductions of drawings and paintings. 279pp. 5⅜ x 8½. 22487-2 Pa. $7.95

DRAWING THE LIVING FIGURE, Joseph Sheppard. Innovative approach to artistic anatomy focuses on specifics of surface anatomy, rather than muscles and bones. Over 170 drawings of live models in front, back and side views, and in widely varying poses. Accompanying diagrams. 177 illustrations. Introduction. Index. 144pp. 8⅜ x11¼. 26723-7 Pa. $8.95

GOTHIC AND OLD ENGLISH ALPHABETS: 100 Complete Fonts, Dan X. Solo. Add power, elegance to posters, signs, other graphics with 100 stunning copyright-free alphabets: Blackstone, Dolbey, Germania, 97 more–including many lower-case, numerals, punctuation marks. 104pp. 8⅛ x 11. 24695-7 Pa. $8.95

HOW TO DO BEADWORK, Mary White. Fundamental book on craft from simple projects to five-bead chains and woven works. 106 illustrations. 142pp. 5⅜ x 8. 20697-1 Pa. $5.95

THE BOOK OF WOOD CARVING, Charles Marshall Sayers. Finest book for beginners discusses fundamentals and offers 34 designs. "Absolutely first rate . . . well thought out and well executed."–E. J. Tangerman. 118pp. 7¾ x 10⅝. 23654-4 Pa. $7.95

ILLUSTRATED CATALOG OF CIVIL WAR MILITARY GOODS: Union Army Weapons, Insignia, Uniform Accessories, and Other Equipment, Schuyler, Hartley, and Graham. Rare, profusely illustrated 1846 catalog includes Union Army uniform and dress regulations, arms and ammunition, coats, insignia, flags, swords, rifles, etc. 226 illustrations. 160pp. 9 x 12. 24939-5 Pa. $10.95

WOMEN'S FASHIONS OF THE EARLY 1900s: An Unabridged Republication of "New York Fashions, 1909," National Cloak & Suit Co. Rare catalog of mail-order fashions documents women's and children's clothing styles shortly after the turn of the century. Captions offer full descriptions, prices. Invaluable resource for fashion, costume historians. Approximately 725 illustrations. 128pp. 8⅜ x 11¼. 27276-1 Pa. $11.95

THE 1912 AND 1915 GUSTAV STICKLEY FURNITURE CATALOGS, Gustav Stickley. With over 200 detailed illustrations and descriptions, these two catalogs are essential reading and reference materials and identification guides for Stickley furniture. Captions cite materials, dimensions and prices. 112pp. 6½ x 9¼. 26676-1 Pa. $9.95

EARLY AMERICAN LOCOMOTIVES, John H. White, Jr. Finest locomotive engravings from early 19th century: historical (1804–74), main-line (after 1870), special, foreign, etc. 147 plates. 142pp. 11⅜ x 8¼. 22772-3 Pa. $10.95

THE TALL SHIPS OF TODAY IN PHOTOGRAPHS, Frank O. Braynard. Lavishly illustrated tribute to nearly 100 majestic contemporary sailing vessels: Amerigo Vespucci, Clearwater, Constitution, Eagle, Mayflower, Sea Cloud, Victory, many more. Authoritative captions provide statistics, background on each ship. 190 black-and-white photographs and illustrations. Introduction. 128pp. 8⅞ x 11¾. 27163-3 Pa. $14.95

LITTLE BOOK OF EARLY AMERICAN CRAFTS AND TRADES, Peter Stockham (ed.). 1807 children's book explains crafts and trades: baker, hatter, cooper, potter, and many others. 23 copperplate illustrations. 140pp. 4⅝ x 6.
23336-7 Pa. $4.95

VICTORIAN FASHIONS AND COSTUMES FROM HARPER'S BAZAR, 1867–1898, Stella Blum (ed.). Day costumes, evening wear, sports clothes, shoes, hats, other accessories in over 1,000 detailed engravings. 320pp. 9⅜ x 12¼.
22990-4 Pa. $15.95

GUSTAV STICKLEY, THE CRAFTSMAN, Mary Ann Smith. Superb study surveys broad scope of Stickley's achievement, especially in architecture. Design philosophy, rise and fall of the Craftsman empire, descriptions and floor plans for many Craftsman houses, more. 86 black-and-white halftones. 31 line illustrations. Introduction 208pp. 6½ x 9¼. 27210-9 Pa. $9.95

THE LONG ISLAND RAIL ROAD IN EARLY PHOTOGRAPHS, Ron Ziel. Over 220 rare photos, informative text document origin (1844) and development of rail service on Long Island. Vintage views of early trains, locomotives, stations, passengers, crews, much more. Captions. 8⅞ x 11¾. 26301-0 Pa. $13.95

VOYAGE OF THE LIBERDADE, Joshua Slocum. Great 19th-century mariner's thrilling, first-hand account of the wreck of his ship off South America, the 35-foot boat he built from the wreckage, and its remarkable voyage home. 128pp. 5⅜ x 8½.
40022-0 Pa. $4.95

TEN BOOKS ON ARCHITECTURE, Vitruvius. The most important book ever written on architecture. Early Roman aesthetics, technology, classical orders, site selection, all other aspects. Morgan translation. 331pp. 5⅜ x 8½. 20645-9 Pa. $8.95

THE HUMAN FIGURE IN MOTION, Eadweard Muybridge. More than 4,500 stopped-action photos, in action series, showing undraped men, women, children jumping, lying down, throwing, sitting, wrestling, carrying, etc. 390pp. 7⅞ x 10⅝.
20204-6 Clothbd. $27.95

TREES OF THE EASTERN AND CENTRAL UNITED STATES AND CANADA, William M. Harlow. Best one-volume guide to 140 trees. Full descriptions, woodlore, range, etc. Over 600 illustrations. Handy size. 288pp. 4½ x 6⅜.
20395-6 Pa. $6.95

SONGS OF WESTERN BIRDS, Dr. Donald J. Borror. Complete song and call repertoire of 60 western species, including flycatchers, juncoes, cactus wrens, many more–includes fully illustrated booklet. Cassette and manual 99913-0 $8.95

GROWING AND USING HERBS AND SPICES, Milo Miloradovich. Versatile handbook provides all the information needed for cultivation and use of all the herbs and spices available in North America. 4 illustrations. Index. Glossary. 236pp. 5⅜ x 8½.
25058-X Pa. $7.95

BIG BOOK OF MAZES AND LABYRINTHS, Walter Shepherd. 50 mazes and labyrinths in all–classical, solid, ripple, and more–in one great volume. Perfect inexpensive puzzler for clever youngsters. Full solutions. 112pp. 8⅛ x 11.
22951-3 Pa. $5.95

PIANO TUNING, J. Cree Fischer. Clearest, best book for beginner, amateur. Simple repairs, raising dropped notes, tuning by easy method of flattened fifths. No previous skills needed. 4 illustrations. 201pp. 5⅜ x 8½. 23267-0 Pa. $6.95

HINTS TO SINGERS, Lillian Nordica. Selecting the right teacher, developing confidence, overcoming stage fright, and many other important skills receive thoughtful discussion in this indispensible guide, written by a world-famous diva of four decades' experience. 96pp. 5⅜ x 8½. 40094-8 Pa. $4.95

THE COMPLETE NONSENSE OF EDWARD LEAR, Edward Lear. All nonsense limericks, zany alphabets, Owl and Pussycat, songs, nonsense botany, etc., illustrated by Lear. Total of 320pp. 5⅜ x 8½. (USO) 20167-8 Pa. $7.95

VICTORIAN PARLOUR POETRY: An Annotated Anthology, Michael R. Turner. 117 gems by Longfellow, Tennyson, Browning, many lesser-known poets. "The Village Blacksmith," "Curfew Must Not Ring Tonight," "Only a Baby Small," dozens more, often difficult to find elsewhere. Index of poets, titles, first lines. xxiii + 325pp. 5⅝ x 8¼. 27044-0 Pa. $8.95

DUBLINERS, James Joyce. Fifteen stories offer vivid, tightly focused observations of the lives of Dublin's poorer classes. At least one, "The Dead," is considered a masterpiece. Reprinted complete and unabridged from standard edition. 160pp. 5$\frac{3}{16}$ x 8¼. 26870-5 Pa. $1.00

GREAT WEIRD TALES: 14 Stories by Lovecraft, Blackwood, Machen and Others, S. T. Joshi (ed.). 14 spellbinding tales, including "The Sin Eater," by Fiona McLeod, "The Eye Above the Mantel," by Frank Belknap Long, as well as renowned works by R. H. Barlow, Lord Dunsany, Arthur Machen, W. C. Morrow and eight other masters of the genre. 256pp. 5⅜ x 8½. (USO) 40436-6 Pa. $8.95

THE BOOK OF THE SACRED MAGIC OF ABRAMELIN THE MAGE, translated by S. MacGregor Mathers. Medieval manuscript of ceremonial magic. Basic document in Aleister Crowley, Golden Dawn groups. 268pp. 5⅜ x 8½. 23211-5 Pa. $9.95

NEW RUSSIAN-ENGLISH AND ENGLISH-RUSSIAN DICTIONARY, M. A. O'Brien. This is a remarkably handy Russian dictionary, containing a surprising amount of information, including over 70,000 entries. 366pp. 4½ x 6⅛. 20208-9 Pa. $10.95

HISTORIC HOMES OF THE AMERICAN PRESIDENTS, Second, Revised Edition, Irvin Haas. A traveler's guide to American Presidential homes, most open to the public, depicting and describing homes occupied by every American President from George Washington to George Bush. With visiting hours, admission charges, travel routes. 175 photographs. Index. 160pp. 8¼ x 11. 26751-2 Pa. $11.95

NEW YORK IN THE FORTIES, Andreas Feininger. 162 brilliant photographs by the well-known photographer, formerly with *Life* magazine. Commuters, shoppers, Times Square at night, much else from city at its peak. Captions by John von Hartz. 181pp. 9¼ x 10¾. 23585-8 Pa. $13.95

INDIAN SIGN LANGUAGE, William Tomkins. Over 525 signs developed by Sioux and other tribes. Written instructions and diagrams. Also 290 pictographs. 111pp. 6⅛ x 9¼. 22029-X Pa. $3.95

ANATOMY: A Complete Guide for Artists, Joseph Sheppard. A master of figure drawing shows artists how to render human anatomy convincingly. Over 460 illustrations. 224pp. 8⅜ x 11¼. 27279-6 Pa. $11.95

MEDIEVAL CALLIGRAPHY: Its History and Technique, Marc Drogin. Spirited history, comprehensive instruction manual covers 13 styles (ca. 4th century thru 15th). Excellent photographs; directions for duplicating medieval techniques with modern tools. 224pp. 8⅜ x 11¼. 26142-5 Pa. $12.95

DRIED FLOWERS: How to Prepare Them, Sarah Whitlock and Martha Rankin. Complete instructions on how to use silica gel, meal and borax, perlite aggregate, sand and borax, glycerine and water to create attractive permanent flower arrangements. 12 illustrations. 32pp. 5⅜ x 8½. 21802-3 Pa. $1.00

EASY-TO-MAKE BIRD FEEDERS FOR WOODWORKERS, Scott D. Campbell. Detailed, simple-to-use guide for designing, constructing, caring for and using feeders. Text, illustrations for 12 classic and contemporary designs. 96pp. 5⅜ x 8½. 25847-5 Pa. $3.95

SCOTTISH WONDER TALES FROM MYTH AND LEGEND, Donald A. Mackenzie. 16 lively tales tell of giants rumbling down mountainsides, of a magic wand that turns stone pillars into warriors, of gods and goddesses, evil hags, powerful forces and more. 240pp. 5⅜ x 8½. 29677-6 Pa. $6.95

THE HISTORY OF UNDERCLOTHES, C. Willett Cunnington and Phyllis Cunnington. Fascinating, well-documented survey covering six centuries of English undergarments, enhanced with over 100 illustrations: 12th-century laced-up bodice, footed long drawers (1795), 19th-century bustles, 19th-century corsets for men, Victorian "bust improvers," much more. 272pp. 5⅜ x 8¼. 27124-2 Pa. $9.95

ARTS AND CRAFTS FURNITURE: The Complete Brooks Catalog of 1912, Brooks Manufacturing Co. Photos and detailed descriptions of more than 150 now very collectible furniture designs from the Arts and Crafts movement depict davenports, settees, buffets, desks, tables, chairs, bedsteads, dressers and more, all built of solid, quarter-sawed oak. Invaluable for students and enthusiasts of antiques, Americana and the decorative arts. 80pp. 6½ x 9¼. 27471-3 Pa. $8.95

WILBUR AND ORVILLE: A Biography of the Wright Brothers, Fred Howard. Definitive, crisply written study tells the full story of the brothers' lives and work. A vividly written biography, unparalleled in scope and color, that also captures the spirit of an extraordinary era. 560pp. 6⅛ x 9¼. 40297-5 Pa. $17.95

THE ARTS OF THE SAILOR: Knotting, Splicing and Ropework, Hervey Garrett Smith. Indispensable shipboard reference covers tools, basic knots and useful hitches; handsewing and canvas work, more. Over 100 illustrations. Delightful reading for sea lovers. 256pp. 5⅜ x 8½. 26440-8 Pa. $8.95

FRANK LLOYD WRIGHT'S FALLINGWATER: The House and Its History, Second, Revised Edition, Donald Hoffmann. A total revision—both in text and illustrations—of the standard document on Fallingwater, the boldest, most personal architectural statement of Wright's mature years, updated with valuable new material from the recently opened Frank Lloyd Wright Archives. "Fascinating"—*The New York Times*. 116 illustrations. 128pp. 9¼ x 10¾. 27430-6 Pa. $12.95

PHOTOGRAPHIC SKETCHBOOK OF THE CIVIL WAR, Alexander Gardner. 100 photos taken on field during the Civil War. Famous shots of Manassas Harper's Ferry, Lincoln, Richmond, slave pens, etc. 244pp. 10⅝ x 8¼.　22731-6 Pa. $10.95

FIVE ACRES AND INDEPENDENCE, Maurice G. Kains. Great back-to-the-land classic explains basics of self-sufficient farming. The one book to get. 95 illustrations. 397pp. 5⅜ x 8½.　20974-1 Pa. $7.95

SONGS OF EASTERN BIRDS, Dr. Donald J. Borror. Songs and calls of 60 species most common to eastern U.S.: warblers, woodpeckers, flycatchers, thrushes, larks, many more in high-quality recording.　Cassette and manual 99912-2 $9.95

A MODERN HERBAL, Margaret Grieve. Much the fullest, most exact, most useful compilation of herbal material. Gigantic alphabetical encyclopedia, from aconite to zedoary, gives botanical information, medical properties, folklore, economic uses, much else. Indispensable to serious reader. 161 illustrations. 888pp. 6½ x 9¼. 2-vol. set. (USO)　Vol. I: 22798-7 Pa. $9.95
Vol. II: 22799-5 Pa. $9.95

HIDDEN TREASURE MAZE BOOK, Dave Phillips. Solve 34 challenging mazes accompanied by heroic tales of adventure. Evil dragons, people-eating plants, bloodthirsty giants, many more dangerous adversaries lurk at every twist and turn. 34 mazes, stories, solutions. 48pp. 8¼ x 11.　24566-7 Pa. $2.95

LETTERS OF W. A. MOZART, Wolfgang A. Mozart. Remarkable letters show bawdy wit, humor, imagination, musical insights, contemporary musical world; includes some letters from Leopold Mozart. 276pp. 5⅜ x 8½.　22859-2 Pa. $7.95

BASIC PRINCIPLES OF CLASSICAL BALLET, Agrippina Vaganova. Great Russian theoretician, teacher explains methods for teaching classical ballet. 118 illustrations. 175pp. 5⅜ x 8½.　22036-2 Pa. $5.95

THE JUMPING FROG, Mark Twain. Revenge edition. The original story of The Celebrated Jumping Frog of Calaveras County, a hapless French translation, and Twain's hilarious "retranslation" from the French. 12 illustrations. 66pp. 5⅜ x 8½.　22686-7 Pa. $3.95

BEST REMEMBERED POEMS, Martin Gardner (ed.). The 126 poems in this superb collection of 19th- and 20th-century British and American verse range from Shelley's "To a Skylark" to the impassioned "Renascence" of Edna St. Vincent Millay and to Edward Lear's whimsical "The Owl and the Pussycat." 224pp. 5⅜ x 8½.
27165-X Pa. $5.95

COMPLETE SONNETS, William Shakespeare. Over 150 exquisite poems deal with love, friendship, the tyranny of time, beauty's evanescence, death and other themes in language of remarkable power, precision and beauty. Glossary of archaic terms. 80pp. 5³⁄₁₆ x 8¼.　26686-9 Pa. $1.00

BODIES IN A BOOKSHOP, R. T. Campbell. Challenging mystery of blackmail and murder with ingenious plot and superbly drawn characters. In the best tradition of British suspense fiction. 192pp. 5⅜ x 8½.　24720-1 Pa. $6.95

THE WIT AND HUMOR OF OSCAR WILDE, Alvin Redman (ed.). More than 1,000 ripostes, paradoxes, wisecracks: Work is the curse of the drinking classes; I can resist everything except temptation; etc. 258pp. 5⅜ x 8½. 20602-5 Pa. $6.95

SHAKESPEARE LEXICON AND QUOTATION DICTIONARY, Alexander Schmidt. Full definitions, locations, shades of meaning in every word in plays and poems. More than 50,000 exact quotations. 1,485pp. 6½ x 9¼. 2-vol. set.
Vol. 1: 22726-X Pa. $17.95
Vol. 2: 22727-8 Pa. $17.95

SELECTED POEMS, Emily Dickinson. Over 100 best-known, best-loved poems by one of America's foremost poets, reprinted from authoritative early editions. No comparable edition at this price. Index of first lines. 64pp. 5³⁄₁₆ x 8¼.
26466-1 Pa. $1.00

THE INSIDIOUS DR. FU-MANCHU, Sax Rohmer. The first of the popular mystery series introduces a pair of English detectives to their archnemesis, the diabolical Dr. Fu-Manchu. Flavorful atmosphere, fast-paced action, and colorful characters enliven this classic of the genre. 208pp. 5³⁄₁₆ x 8¼. 29898-1 Pa. $2.00

THE MALLEUS MALEFICARUM OF KRAMER AND SPRENGER, translated by Montague Summers. Full text of most important witchhunter's "bible," used by both Catholics and Protestants. 278pp. 6⅝ x 10. 22802-9 Pa. $12.95

SPANISH STORIES/CUENTOS ESPAÑOLES: A Dual-Language Book, Angel Flores (ed.). Unique format offers 13 great stories in Spanish by Cervantes, Borges, others. Faithful English translations on facing pages. 352pp. 5⅜ x 8½.
25399-6 Pa. $8.95

GARDEN CITY, LONG ISLAND, IN EARLY PHOTOGRAPHS, 1869–1919, Mildred H. Smith. Handsome treasury of 118 vintage pictures, accompanied by carefully researched captions, document the Garden City Hotel fire (1899), the Vanderbilt Cup Race (1908), the first airmail flight departing from the Nassau Boulevard Aerodrome (1911), and much more. 96pp. 8⅞ x 11¾. 40669-5 Pa. $12.95

OLD QUEENS, N.Y., IN EARLY PHOTOGRAPHS, Vincent F. Seyfried and William Asadorian. Over 160 rare photographs of Maspeth, Jamaica, Jackson Heights, and other areas. Vintage views of DeWitt Clinton mansion, 1939 World's Fair and more. Captions. 192pp. 8⅞ x 11. 26358-4 Pa. $12.95

CAPTURED BY THE INDIANS: 15 Firsthand Accounts, 1750-1870, Frederick Drimmer. Astounding true historical accounts of grisly torture, bloody conflicts, relentless pursuits, miraculous escapes and more, by people who lived to tell the tale. 384pp. 5⅜ x 8½. 24901-8 Pa. $8.95

THE WORLD'S GREAT SPEECHES (Fourth Enlarged Edition), Lewis Copeland, Lawrence W. Lamm, and Stephen J. McKenna. Nearly 300 speeches provide public speakers with a wealth of updated quotes and inspiration–from Pericles' funeral oration and William Jennings Bryan's "Cross of Gold Speech" to Malcolm X's powerful words on the Black Revolution and Earl of Spenser's tribute to his sister, Diana, Princess of Wales. 944pp. 5⅜ x 8⅜. 40903-1 Pa. $15.95

THE BOOK OF THE SWORD, Sir Richard F. Burton. Great Victorian scholar/adventurer's eloquent, erudite history of the "queen of weapons"–from prehistory to early Roman Empire. Evolution and development of early swords, variations (sabre, broadsword, cutlass, scimitar, etc.), much more. 336pp. 6⅛ x 9¼.
25434-8 Pa. $9.95

AUTOBIOGRAPHY: The Story of My Experiments with Truth, Mohandas K. Gandhi. Boyhood, legal studies, purification, the growth of the Satyagraha (nonviolent protest) movement. Critical, inspiring work of the man responsible for the freedom of India. 480pp. 5⅜ x 8½. (USO) 24593-4 Pa. $8.95

CELTIC MYTHS AND LEGENDS, T. W. Rolleston. Masterful retelling of Irish and Welsh stories and tales. Cuchulain, King Arthur, Deirdre, the Grail, many more. First paperback edition. 58 full-page illustrations. 512pp. 5⅜ x 8½. 26507-2 Pa. $9.95

THE PRINCIPLES OF PSYCHOLOGY, William James. Famous long course complete, unabridged. Stream of thought, time perception, memory, experimental methods; great work decades ahead of its time. 94 figures. 1,391pp. 5⅜ x 8½. 2-vol. set.
Vol. I: 20381-6 Pa. $13.95
Vol. II: 20382-4 Pa. $14.95

THE WORLD AS WILL AND REPRESENTATION, Arthur Schopenhauer. Definitive English translation of Schopenhauer's life work, correcting more than 1,000 errors, omissions in earlier translations. Translated by E. F. J. Payne. Total of 1,269pp. 5⅜ x 8½. 2-vol. set.
Vol. 1: 21761-2 Pa. $12.95
Vol. 2: 21762-0 Pa. $12.95

MAGIC AND MYSTERY IN TIBET, Madame Alexandra David-Neel. Experiences among lamas, magicians, sages, sorcerers, Bonpa wizards. A true psychic discovery. 32 illustrations. 321pp. 5⅜ x 8½. (USO) 22682-4 Pa. $9.95

THE EGYPTIAN BOOK OF THE DEAD, E. A. Wallis Budge. Complete reproduction of Ani's papyrus, finest ever found. Full hieroglyphic text, interlinear transliteration, word-for-word translation, smooth translation. 533pp. 6½ x 9¼.
21866-X Pa. $11.95

MATHEMATICS FOR THE NONMATHEMATICIAN, Morris Kline. Detailed, college-level treatment of mathematics in cultural and historical context, with numerous exercises. Recommended Reading Lists. Tables. Numerous figures. 641pp. 5⅜ x 8½.
24823-2 Pa. $11.95

PROBABILISTIC METHODS IN THE THEORY OF STRUCTURES, Isaac Elishakoff. Well-written introduction covers the elements of the theory of probability from two or more random variables, the reliability of such multivariable structures, the theory of random function, Monte Carlo methods of treating problems incapable of exact solution, and more. Examples. 502pp. 5³/₈ x 8¹/₂. 40691-1 Pa. $16.95

THE RIME OF THE ANCIENT MARINER, Gustave Doré, S. T. Coleridge. Doré's finest work; 34 plates capture moods, subtleties of poem. Flawless full-size reproductions printed on facing pages with authoritative text of poem. "Beautiful. Simply beautiful."–Publisher's Weekly. 77pp. 9¼ x 12. 22305-1 Pa. $7.95

NORTH AMERICAN INDIAN DESIGNS FOR ARTISTS AND CRAFTSPEOPLE, Eva Wilson. Over 360 authentic copyright-free designs adapted from Navajo blankets, Hopi pottery, Sioux buffalo hides, more. Geometrics, symbolic figures, plant and animal motifs, etc. 128pp. 8⅜ x 11. (EUK) 25341-4 Pa. $8.95

SCULPTURE: Principles and Practice, Louis Slobodkin. Step-by-step approach to clay, plaster, metals, stone; classical and modern. 253 drawings, photos. 255pp. 8⅛ x 11.
22960-2 Pa. $11.95

THE INFLUENCE OF SEA POWER UPON HISTORY, 1660–1783, A. T. Mahan. Influential classic of naval history and tactics still used as text in war colleges. First paperback edition. 4 maps. 24 battle plans. 640pp. 5⅜ x 8½.   25509-3 Pa. $14.95

THE STORY OF THE TITANIC AS TOLD BY ITS SURVIVORS, Jack Winocour (ed.). What it was really like. Panic, despair, shocking inefficiency, and a little heroism. More thrilling than any fictional account. 26 illustrations. 320pp. 5⅜ x 8½.   20610-6 Pa. $8.95

FAIRY AND FOLK TALES OF THE IRISH PEASANTRY, William Butler Yeats (ed.). Treasury of 64 tales from the twilight world of Celtic myth and legend: "The Soul Cages," "The Kildare Pooka," "King O'Toole and his Goose," many more. Introduction and Notes by W. B. Yeats. 352pp. 5⅜ x 8½.   26941-8 Pa. $8.95

BUDDHIST MAHAYANA TEXTS, E. B. Cowell and Others (eds.). Superb, accurate translations of basic documents in Mahayana Buddhism, highly important in history of religions. The Buddha-karita of Asvaghosha, Larger Sukhavativyuha, more. 448pp. 5⅜ x 8½.   25552-2 Pa. $12.95

ONE TWO THREE . . . INFINITY: Facts and Speculations of Science, George Gamow. Great physicist's fascinating, readable overview of contemporary science: number theory, relativity, fourth dimension, entropy, genes, atomic structure, much more. 128 illustrations. Index. 352pp. 5⅜ x 8½.   25664-2 Pa. $8.95

EXPERIMENTATION AND MEASUREMENT, W. J. Youden. Introductory manual explains laws of measurement in simple terms and offers tips for achieving accuracy and minimizing errors. Mathematics of measurement, use of instruments, experimenting with machines. 1994 edition. Foreword. Preface. Introduction. Epilogue. Selected Readings. Glossary. Index. Tables and figures. 128pp. 5³/₈ x 8¹/₂.   40451-X Pa. $6.95

DALÍ ON MODERN ART: The Cuckolds of Antiquated Modern Art, Salvador Dalí. Influential painter skewers modern art and its practitioners. Outrageous evaluations of Picasso, Cézanne, Turner, more. 15 renderings of paintings discussed. 44 calligraphic decorations by Dalí. 96pp. 5⅜ x 8½. (USO)   29220-7 Pa. $5.95

ANTIQUE PLAYING CARDS: A Pictorial History, Henry René D'Allemagne. Over 900 elaborate, decorative images from rare playing cards (14th–20th centuries): Bacchus, death, dancing dogs, hunting scenes, royal coats of arms, players cheating, much more. 96pp. 9¼ x 12¼.   29265-7 Pa. $12.95

MAKING FURNITURE MASTERPIECES: 30 Projects with Measured Drawings, Franklin H. Gottshall. Step-by-step instructions, illustrations for constructing handsome, useful pieces, among them a Sheraton desk, Chippendale chair, Spanish desk, Queen Anne table and a William and Mary dressing mirror. 224pp. 8⅛ x 11¼.   29338-6 Pa. $13.95

THE FOSSIL BOOK: A Record of Prehistoric Life, Patricia V. Rich et al. Profusely illustrated definitive guide covers everything from single-celled organisms and dinosaurs to birds and mammals and the interplay between climate and man. Over 1,500 illustrations. 760pp. 7½ x 10⅛.   29371-8 Pa. $29.95

Prices subject to change without notice.

Available at your book dealer or write for free catalog to Dept. GI, Dover Publications, Inc., 31 East 2nd St., Mineola, N.Y. 11501. Dover publishes more than 500 books each year on science, elementary and advanced mathematics, biology, music, art, literary history, social sciences and other areas.